GERMANY
Practical Commercial Law

DR MICHAEL H BÖCKER
Rechtsanwälte Sottung, Ulsenheimer, Schlüter, Böcker und Partner, Munich
BABETTE MÄRZHEUSER
Rechtsanwältin and Legal Assistant with Withers Solicitors, London
MICHAEL NUSSER
Rechtsanwalt in Munich
KATHARINA SCHEJA
Sottung, Ulsenheimer, Schlüter, Böcker und Partner, Munich

GENERAL EDITOR
ALEXIS MAITLAND HUDSON
Avocat à la cour
Solicitor

LONGMAN

Published by
Longman Law, Tax and Finance
Longman Group UK Ltd
21–27 Lamb's Conduit Street
London WC1N 3NJ

Associated offices
Australia, Hong Kong, Malaysia, Singapore, USA

ISBN 0851 217745

A CIP catalogue record for this book is available from the British Library.

Typeset by Servis Filmsetting Ltd, Manchester

Printed and bound in Great Britain by Biddles Ltd, Guildford, Surrey

CONTENTS

Page

Introduction 1
- General 1
- Sources of Law 1
- Unification 2
- Courts 3
  - Civil Courts 3
  - Labour Courts 4
  - Administrative Courts 4
  - Constitutional Courts 4
- Civil Procedure 5
- Rechtsanwälte (German lawyers) 5
- Notaries 6

Chapter One: Commercial and Intellectual Property 7
- 1.1 Introduction 7
- 1.2 Patents 8
  - 1.2.1 Novelty 8
  - 1.2.2 Utility 8
  - 1.2.3 Patent Procedural Law 9
  - 1.2.4 Legal Remedies against a Patent Registration 10
- 1.3 Utility patents 11
  - 1.3.1 New Design 12
  - 1.3.2 Utility Purpose 12
  - 1.3.3 Movable Objects 12
  - 1.3.4 Novelty 12
  - 1.3.5 Procedure 12
  - 1.3.6 Double Protection 13
  - 1.3.7 Collisions 14
- 1.4 Registered Designs 14
  - 1.4.1 Registered Designs Law 14

1.4.2 Requirements for Registration 14
1.4.3 Registration Procedure 15
1.4.4 Appeals and other Remedies 16
1.4.5 Scope of Protection 16
1.5 Copyrights 16
1.5.1 Copyright Law 16
1.5.2 Characteristics of a Copyright 16
1.5.3 Protection Offered by Copyright Law 18
1.5.4 Restrictions and Expiry 19
1.5.5 Transfer of Copyright 20
1.6 Protection of Names, Labels and Trademarks 21
1.6.1 Definition of a Trademark 22
1.6.2 Priority Rule 23
1.6.3 Registration Procedure 24
1.6.4 Objection Procedure and other Remedies 25
1.6.5 Scope of Protection 25
1.6.6 Goodwill Protection 25

Chapter Two: Competition Law 27
2.1 Introduction 27
2.2 The Law of Unfair Competition (UWG) 28
2.2.1 Article 1 29
2.2.2 Article 3 31
2.2.3 Impact of the European Advertising Directive on German Law (Directive 84/850) 34
2.2.4 Courses of Action Arising out of Unfair Competition Law 35
2.2.5 Procedual Peculiarities 35
2.3 Cartels, Monopolies and Mergers 35
2.3.1 Authorities 36
2.3.2 Procedures 36
2.4 The Contents of German Cartels Law 37
2.4.1 The Definition of a Cartel 38
2.4.2 Privileged Cartels 41
2.4.3 Vertical Agreements 43
2.4.4 Comparison to EEC Law 46
2.5 Companies which Dominate the Market 47
2.5.1 Abuse of Market Power 47
2.5.2 Dominant Position on the Market 48
2.5.3 European Law 48

2.5.4 Courses of Action 49
2.6 Merger Control 49
2.6.1 The System of Fusion Control 50
2.6.2 Notification Procedure 51

Chapter Three: Business Organisation and Company Formation 52
3.1 Introduction 52
3.2 Partnerships and Sole Traders 53
3.2.1 Sole Traders 53
3.2.2 Partnerships 55
3.2.3 Limited Partnerships 57
3.2.4 Silent Partnerships 60
3.3 Limited Companies and Public Limited Companies 61
3.3.1 GmbH (Limited Company) 61
3.3.2 The AG (Public Limited Company) 64
3.3.3 VVaG and eG, Reederei 68
3.4 The EEIG 69
3.5 Disclosure Provisions 70

Chapter Four: Mergers and Acquisitions 72
4.1 Introduction 72
4.2 The Object of a Company Purchase 72
4.3 The Purchase of Assets 73
4.4 The Purchase of a Holding 75
4.4.1 Holdings and Legal Entities 75
4.4.2 Holdings and Partnerships 75
4.5 Additional Considerations for a Company Purchase 76
4.5.1 Supervision of Mergers 76
4.5.2 Fiscal Considerations 76
4.5.3 Licences 76
4.5.4 Letter of Intent 77
4.6 Liability 77
4.6.1 Liability for Continuation of Company Name 77
4.6.2 Liability According to Art 419 of the Civil Code 78
4.6.3 Purchaser's Liability for Unpaid Taxes 78
4.6.4 Partnership Shares 78
4.6.5 GmbH Shares and Stocks 79
4.7 Guarantees 79

4.7.1 Statutory Law 79
4.7.2 Contractual Guarantees 80

Chapter Five: Agency, Franchising and Related Distribution Contracts 81
5.1 Introduction 81
5.2 Agency 81
5.2.1 Branches 82
5.2.2 Commercial Representatives 82
5.2.3 Commission Agents 85
5.2.4 Brokers 85
5.3 Franchise Contracts 86
5.3.1 The Applicable Law 87
5.3.2 Terms of the Contract 87
5.3.3 Termination 88
5.3.4 Industrial Property Protection for Franchise System? 88
5.3.5 EEC Law 89
5.4 Other Forms of Distribution 89
5.4.1 Home Traders 89
5.4.2 Foreign Companies 91

Chapter Six: Property and Succession 92
6.1 Introduction 92
6.2 Property Law 92
6.2.1 Sale of Movable Objects 93
6.2.2 Real Property 94
6.2.3 Co-property 98
6.2.4 Business Leases 98
6.3 Succession 99
6.3.1 Types of Succession 100
6.3.2 Inheritance Tax 102

Chapter Seven: Immigration and Employment 103
7.1 Immigration 103
7.1.1 Non-EEC Nationals 103
7.1.2 EEC Nationals 104
7.2 Employment Law 104
7.2.1 Employment Contracts 105
7.2.2 Termination 107

7.2.3 Employee Co-determination 110
7.2.4 Trade Unions and Collective Bargaining 111
7.2.5 Discrimination 113
7.2.6 Labour Courts 113

Chapter Eight: Taxation Law 114
8.1 Introduction 114
8.2 Direct Taxes 115
8.2.1 Income Tax 115
8.2.2 Corporation Tax 117
8.2.3 Capital Tax 118
8.2.4 Inheritance Tax 119
8.2.5 Trade Tax 120
8.3 Indirect Taxes 120
8.3.1 Value Added Tax 121
8.3.2 Other Indirect Taxes 122
8.3.3 Special Contributions 123

Chapter Nine: Environmental and Planning Law 124
9.1 Introduction 124
9.2 Basic German Public Law 124
9.2.1 Administrative Structures 124
9.2.2 Administrative Orders 125
9.2.3 Federal and Non-Federal Laws 125
9.3 Building Law 126
9.3.1 Building Areas 126
9.3.2 Building Ordinance 126
9.3.3 Neighbour Rights 127
9.3.4 Procedure 127
9.3.5 Large Projects 127
9.4 Environmental Protection 128
9.4.1 Licensing 128
9.4.2 Control of Unlicensed Businesses 129
9.5 Water and Waste Law 129
9.5.1 Water Law 129
9.5.2 Waste Disposal Law 130
9.6 Environmental Liability Law 130
9.6.1 Hazardous Plants 131
9.6.2 Liability 131

9.7 Product Labelling 132
9.7.1 Foodstuffs 132
9.7.2 Cosmetics 133
9.7.3 EEC Law 133

Chapter Ten: Financing 134
10.1 Introduction 134
10.2 Loans 134
10.2.1 Conclusion of a Loans Contract 135
10.2.2 Building Society Savings Plans 135
10.2.3 Private Loans 135
10.2.4 Terms and Conditions 136
10.2.5 Securities 137
10.3 Leasing 138
10.3.1 Finance Leasing 139
10.3.2 Operating Leasing 140
10.3.3 Real Estate Leasing 140
10.4 Giving Credit to Customers 140
10.4.1 Consumer Credit 140
10.4.2 Third Party Finance 141
10.4.3 Retention of Title 141

Chapter Eleven: Insolvency and Enforcement 142
11.1 Introduction 142
11.2 Enforcement 142
11.2.1 Title 142
11.2.2 Methods of Enforcement 144
11.2.3 Procedure 145
11.2.4 Locating Hidden Assets 146
11.3 Insolvency 147
11.3.1 Liquidation Procedure 148
11.3.2 Composition 148
11.3.3 Ranking of Creditors 149
11.3.4 Bankruptcy of the Insolvency Laws 151

Legislation Table 153

Index 155

INTRODUCTION

GENERAL

This book is intended to introduce the legal petitioner to German commercial law. German law was widely codified in the 19th century and, like all codes of law that are based on Roman law, it is arranged into a clearly defined system, leaving the legal petitioner room to manoeuvre only within that system. Thus every legal code will initially state the general rule of law prior to dealing with specific problems. Ways to interpret the law are clearly defined and it is the lawyer's main task to interpret the legal codes according to the four classical Roman rules of deduction; namely the historical, grammatical, teleological and analogical rules. Unlike the case in the UK he is not bound by precedent and, as a result, he may very well succeed in convincing a court to deviate from a decision of the Federal Court of Justice on an important legal point. It has to be noted, however, that the answer which German law will ultimately give to a legal question often corresponds to the one given by English law. Accordingly the differences between the two legal systems are not to be overestimated.

SOURCES OF LAW

When dealing with a legal problem in German law the crucially important initial task is to discover the correct source of law. The most important German law in the sphere of commercial law can be found in *Schönfelder*, published by Beck in Munich. It is a compilation of civil codifications containing over 100 different laws which are numbered and arranged according to topic. The most important ones are:

- BGB —Civil Code (No 20).
- HGB—Commercial Code (No 50).
- ZPO —Code of Civil Procedure (No 100).

In addition to such general codes, there is a vast abundance of smaller commercially relevant codes such as:

- GWB & UWG—Cartel and competition codes.
- GmbHG —Code governing the foundation of limited companies.
- AG —Code governing the formation of public companies.

All these codes deal with special problems relevant only in one particular area of the law.

The languages of such codes is often complicated and ambiguous. To get a better insight into their range of application it is therefore helpful to consult the so-called commentaries. Commentaries provide a systematic explanation of the individual legal provisions, references to important judgments and publications. The most well-known commentaries are:

- BGB —Palandt.
- HGB—Baumbach/Duden/Hopt.
- ZPO —Zoeller.

To be able to use those books correctly it is essential to know the relevant rule of law applicable to a legal problem. In the case of the BGB which contains over 2,300 Articles this may not be an easy task.

UNIFICATION

The political reunification of Germany has given rise to a number of significant peculiarities. On 3 October 1990 the former GDR acceded to the Federal Republic of Germany. As a result the West German legal system has become the law in force in the territory of the former GDR. However, with a view to alleviating difficulties of adaption, special transitional legal provisions are to apply to the area of the former GDR, in some instances for a number of years. A detailed account of such provisions can be found in the annexes to the Treaty of Unification.

Courts

The administration of justice in Germany is characterised by the existence of five separate sets of courts, each having jurisdiction over individual areas of law. Thus, there are civil courts, general and special administrative courts and labour courts — a concept which will often lead to difficulties in establishing the correct jurisdiction.

Civil courts

Most commercial matters would fall within the jurisdiction of the civil courts, which are traditionally divided into four regional units.

At first instance, small claims are brought to the lowest civil court, the *Amtsgericht*, however, claims involving a value in excess of DM 6,000 have to be brought in the regional court, the *Landgericht*, where each party has to be represented by a German lawyer who is admitted at that particular court. The *Landgericht* has a special chamber for commercial cases which, on request, deals with proceedings between merchants and other urgent commercial matters. Such request should usually be made as the commercial chambers are known to work more quickly and effectively than the general civil chambers.

Furthermore, commercial parties are, in principle, allowed to make agreements conferring jurisdiction for disputes concerning property from one regional court to another, if certain other requirements are satisfied. This provision is of interest mainly for contracts between commercial companies, because it enables them to choose a convenient forum rather than having to sue an opponent at the court of his seat.

Appeals can be made against both the decisions of the *Amtsgericht* and the *Landgericht*. It has to be noted, however, that the amount at issue has to come to DM 1,200 in order to be granted leave to appeal. A further appeal to the Federal Court of Justice (*Bundesgerichtshof*) on points of law is possible against decisions of the Court of Appeal (*Oberlandes gericht*) in cases involving an amount greater than DM 60,000, or in disputes concerning matters of fundamental importance. No further remedy exists against decisions of the small claims court.

Labour courts

Labour courts have jurisdiction over disputes concerning labour law. These include, amongst others, disputes arising out of the relationship between employer and employee or claims relating to protection against dismissal and disputes related to strikes and other actions by trade unions.

The appeal system is three-tiered, with two regional courts in every German *Land* and a Federal Labour Court which determines appeals on points of law for the whole country. Parties must be legally represented before the Federal Court. They can also be represented by representatives of trade unions before the other labour courts.

Administrative courts

Administrative courts determine disputes relating to the acts of public authorities.

There are specialised social courts dealing with such acts if they are related to social matters and finance courts, which determine appeals against acts of the fiscal authorities, such as tax bills and tax refunds. General administrative matters, including *inter alia* building permits, commercial licensing and other issues relating to the control public authorities exercise over businesses, are dealt with by general administrative courts. There is again a three-tiered court structure with a possibility of two appeals, the second of which has to be on a point of law and is decided by a federal court.

Constitutional courts

As a last resort and 'fourth instance' Germany has a Federal Constitutional Court. Anybody can bring a formal case in this court against an infringement of his constitutional rights through an act of public authorities. In this context, Acts of Parliament and Acts of German courts are included so that there is always a possibility to challenge a new law or a final judgment as unconstitutional if human rights are at issue.

The Constitutional Court has power to declare any law or judgment null and void, a power that has been called for quite frequently in connection with property rights when public restrictions on business activities were involved.

Civil procedure

German civil procedural law is based on the principle of party autonomy.

Each party is expected to present the full facts of his case and all evidence relating to such facts without request by the courts. The truth of the alleged facts need only be ascertained if the opposing party disputes them and evidence is adduced only if it has been offered by one party. Thus, a claim that is not supported by a detailed account of all relevant events can be dismissed immediately and, consequently, great care has to be taken when drafting a writ.

Unlike dealings in English courts, German judicial procedure is mainly conducted by way of written documents. A recent amendment to the Code of Civil Procedure even allows the court to order a witness to reply in writing to a question of evidence. Other elements of German civil procedure, such as the possibility of applications for judgment in default or injunctions, are similar to the procedure in the UK.

Defendants are provided with leaflets containing instructions by the court on formal requirements of a valid defence. It has to be pointed out that judgment in default can be given against any defendant who is not represented by a German lawyer admitted at the court in question. It is therefore a matter of vital importance to instruct solicitors as soon as a writ is served on a party.

Rechtsanwälte (German lawyers)

Finally a brief paragraph should be dedicated to the rules that govern the legal profession in Germany. Germany has a joint bar, requiring a *Rechtsanwalt* to fulfil both the duties of a barrister and a solicitor. Germany has a regional bar with each *Rechtsanwalt* having the right of audience before one *Landgericht*. Thus, a lawyer admitted at the Landgericht Bonn, for example, can only represent parties which wish to bring or defend a civil action there. The professional provision of legal advice by any other person is in principle prohibited. The fee structure of German law firms is governed by a legal code ('BRAGO', printed in the *Schönfelder* collection) which defines exactly what may be charged for a legal service. Broadly speaking the fees are related to the values involved, rather than to the time spent on a particular case. Thus DM 10,000 may be earned in one hour if property worth DM 1,000,000 is sold. Other fee arrangements are, however, permitted if the party and the German lawyer agree in writing on a fee in excess of what is prescribed or on an hourly fee. In the event of judicial proceedings the unsuccessful party is required to refund all legal expenses incurred by the successful party (costs plus lawyers fees).

NOTARIES

A notary is an independent public officer, often a trained lawyer, whose assistance is needed for the completion of various legal transactions, which are considered to be of outstanding importance. The involvement of a notary is essential for the setting up of businesses because both the purchase of land and the formation of a limited company needs to be attested by a notary public. Otherwise the contract concerned would not be valid in Germany.

Notaries' fees are also governed by a legal code.

1
COMMERCIAL AND INTELLECTUAL PROPERTY

1.1 INTRODUCTION

In Germany the protection of commercial property is governed by a number of different laws, all of which are published in the *Schönfelder* collection. These laws are:

(1) The Patent Law, which protects major technical inventions, such as a brand new piece of machinery or new chemical processes, for a period of 20 years.

(2) The Utility Patent Law, which protects innovations and improvements, such as an improved design of corkscrew or tool with a different shape, for a period of eight years.

(3) The Registered Designs Law, which protects aesthetic designs, for example jewellery, for a period of three years.

(4) The Trademark Law, which protects brands and brand symbols, including names and logos such as 'BMW' or the Longman ship, for a period of 70 years.

(5) Articles 16 and 17 of the UWG (the law of unfair competition), which protect business secrets for an unlimited period of time.

(6) The Copyright Law, which protects intellectual creations, such as works of literature, science and art, on a non-commercial level for a period of 70 years.

All commercial protective rights require registration with the German patent office in Munich to be valid. Specialist patent lawyers with additional training in natural sciences and engineering are available and, because of their special training and technical knowledge, it is highly advisable to consult them in patent matters. Special patent courts exist to deal with legal actions involving decisions of the Patent Office or involving infringements of patented rights.

1.2 Patents

A German patent protects an invention for a period of 20 years from unlicensed production, sale and use. If a patent is violated the holder of the patent has an action for discontinuance and compensation.

A foreign inventor can protect his product in Germany in accordance with the Paris Union Agreement, if his invention meets all the requirements set up by the German Patent Law, which shall be examined in greater detail below.

A patent can only be issued for an **invention**, which is both **new** and **commercially applicable**.

1.2.1 Novelty

The main requirement for the classification of a product as an invention is its novelty. Article 3 of the Patent Law gives a negative definition of novelty, stating that knowledge which is already accessible to the public cannot be considered a novelty. This includes all facts published or described anywhere in the world in the period of time before an application for a patent has been made. Obviously products that have already been patented elsewhere cannot be patented again. There is, however, a period of grace of six months for inventors during which they can decide whether to apply for a patent or not without damaging the 'novelty' status of their product by exhibiting (Patent Law, Art 3) or describing it (Patent Law, Art 4) publicly.

1.2.2 Utility

An invention is also characterised by its utility. This means that it has to be based on a repeatable technical idea which allows the solution to a technical problem. Therefore aesthetic shapes or plans cannot be registered as an invention, the same being true for scientific theories, ideas for games or business concepts.

Inventive work has to overcome a general prejudice by its unexpected or surprising results. In addition to the classical 'one off' new creation (such as the first bicycle), this can also be achieved by transferring a well-known solution from one field of technology to another.

Foods, stimulants and pharmaceuticals may also constitute

a technical invention. Microbiological processes can be protected, with the notable exception of genetically manipulated animals. Plants are protected by a specialised law. A wealth of precedents exists on these matters which can be looked up in a commentary to the Patent Law.

1.2.3 PATENT PROCEDURAL LAW

A patent protects the patented invention for a period of 20 years. To be granted a patent the following procedural requirements have to be met.

Formal requirements of application

A written application to the German Patent Office in Munich must be made. This application has to comply with certain formal requirements. Amongst other points the application needs to contain a detailed description of the invention. It is very important to fulfil this requirement with great care as the description determines the scope of protection. Therefore the invention must be fully disclosed. Drawings of the invented product have to be submitted, or the application will be rejected.

Examination procedure

In contrast to many foreign countries, the German Patent Office will actually examine the invention upon application by an interested party. If such an examination has not been made within a period of seven years after the granting of the patent, the patent will expire without further notice. The purpose of this regulation is to give the inventor time to see whether his invention will be a practical success. It is a statistical fact that only ten per cent of registered inventions actually gain commercial importance.

Examination of obvious flaws

Without an examination application the patent office will only check the patent request for obvious flaws. An application can be rejected on the grounds that it does not meet the formal requirements of the patent law. An obvious flaw would be an insufficient description of the invention or the failure to provide any drawings of it. An obvious lack of inventive merit will also lead to rejection of the application. Thus, an application to have a typewriter or a tape recorder patented would be rejected, because it would be obvious without further research that such items have already been invented.

Applicant

According to German law a patent is issued only to the inventor himself. Only he or a person who has purchased the invention from him may register the invention. However, the patent office does not check whether the applicant is the true inventor unless an objection is raised against him. There is a deadline of three months from the date of the publication of the patent for the presentation of such objections. If no objections are raised, the patent will be issued to the person who registered it first (principle of priority). It follows that quick registration can improve the position of an applicant considerably. It is obviously advantageous to be in a position where others have to raise objections against one's own rights, rather than having to attack the rights of a rival inventor before a patent court.

Inspection of files

The Registry is a public registry and anyone can be granted permission to inspect files, models and samples relating to a particular invention after the expiry of 18 months from the date of application. After this time the files will also be published by the Patent Office in a specialised newspaper called the *Patentblatt*.

Fees

The Patent Office charges fees for registrations, examinations, and other official acts. The application fee currently (1991) stands at DM 100. The registration costs an additional DM 400. After a patent has been issued, yearly fees are chargeable. Failure to pay such fees will result in withdrawal of the patent protection.

1.2.4 LEGAL REMEDIES AGAINST A PATENT REGISTRATION

The German Patent Law provides for various ways of opposing a patent.

Novelty examination

A person who wishes to oppose a patent registration can

apply for an examination of the novelty of the invention. This will lead to an investigation which might reveal that the invention has in fact been described before. If the applicant succeeds with his application, the patent is withdrawn by the Patent Office.

Further and more detailed examination

A request can be made for further and more detailed examination of all requirements of the Patent Law.

As mentioned above the Patent Office usually restricts itself to the control of obvious and grave flaws. Upon application, for which a fee of DM 400 is chargeable, the Patent Office reviews the inventor's submissions in full detail. This process relates to all questions of formal and substantive law and it is quite likely to bring a flaw in a patent application to light.

Action for recovery

A person whose invention has been patented by someone else, has an action for recovery against that person. He can ask for the formal transfer of the patent from the false inventor to himself.

Appeal

Within a period of three months after the publication of a patent there is a right of appeal for any interested party. The appeal has to be made in writing to the Patent Office and must contain full detail of the grounds that the appeal is based on. There is a further appeal against the decision of the Patent Office to the Federal Patent Court. This court can grant leave to appeal on points of law to the Federal Court of Justice.

Revocation

The Patent Office may revoke a patent without corresponding third party application, if it is revealed that a patent should not have been issued in the first place. An informal suggestion to the Patent Office to revoke a patent can be made.

1.3 UTILITY PATENTS

The utility patent, like the patent, requires an invention. However, the requirements on inventive merit are lower. In accordance with Art 1 of the Utility Patent Law only one inventive step concerning a tool or other utility object is needed. The lower inventive merit is reflected in a shorter protection period of only eight years.

1.3.1 New design

A utility patent is characterised by the creation of a new shape or arrangement such as an inventive design, device or circuit. A new object need not necessarily be created. A typical example would be the creation of a new shape for a tool that improves or shortens a working process. Electrical, opto-electrical, pneumatic and hydraulic circuits are also protected as are area patterns and new arrangements for well-known shapes.

1.3.2 Utility purpose

A purely aesthetic purpose will not suffice to qualify a new tool for a utility patent. There needs to be a practical improvement. Thus, a more beautiful design for an object cannot be protected under the Utility Patent Law (it can however be a registered design).

1.3.3 Movable objects

Immovable objects, such as bridges, cannot be protected by a utility patent, although large and complicated machines are included as well as semi-finished products.

1.3.4 Novelty

A utility patent, like a patent, requires the novelty of the invention. However, the difference to similar products which are already known publicly need not be as considerable as in the case of a patent. The novelty effect is only damaged if public use of the invention has been permitted before making an application for a utility patent. A six-month period of grace is granted during which publications of the invention will be disregarded.

1.3.5 Procedure

The procedural requirements that have to be observed when applying for a utility patent are very similar to the ones set up by the Patent Law.

Application

In brief outline there needs to be a written application containing:

(1) a brief technical description of the invention;
(2) a drawing of the new shape; and
(3) the name of the applicant.

Payment of an application fee of DM 50 is also required.

In contrast to the Patent Law, no examination procedures exist. Neither the novelty of the product nor its inventive merit are checked by the Patent Office. It follows that, at this stage, the application can only fail if it neither concerns a tool nor a utility object (eg an application to be granted a patent for the invention of a new breed of dog).

Examination procedure and remedies

A detailed examination of a utility patent will take place if a request for novelty examination is put in.

There is also a general possibility of an appeal to the Patent Court against decisions of the Patent Office.

Finally, any interested party can apply for deletion of a utility patent on the grounds that the patented object does not fulfil the legal requirements set out by the law. If the owner of the patent does not oppose the application for deletion his right will automatically be eliminated.

1.3.6 DOUBLE PROTECTION

Double protection of an invention is possible. If a product fulfils both the characteristics of a patent and a utility patent it can be registered twice. This can be particularly helpful when the success of the patent application is doubtful. The weaker protection of a utility patent can be obtained almost immediately, as there is no examination of the application. However, the inventor must not delay his patent application, as the disclosure of the utility patent to the public by the Patent Office would damage the novelty effect. It is, therefore, advisable to submit both applications at the same time.

Another way of obtaining double protection is to apply for an auxiliary utility patent to cover the period until the patent is issued. Once the patent has been granted it will take priority over the utility patent.

1.3.7 Collisions

Since utility patents are issued without examination of the merits of an application, collisions with a patent can occur. The general collision rule is the priority rule. Thus, the older utility patent will take priority over the younger patent. The owner of the patent will therefore have to come to an agreement with the owner of the utility patent or request the deletion of the utility patent.

1.4 Registered designs

In a modern industrialised society the shape of products has become a major sales factor. Some commercial designs for furniture or household objects are developed by well-known artists or designers which increases the value of a product considerably. For this reason the Registered Designs Law provides an opportunity to protect aesthetic commercial work through registration. Additionally, the Copyright Law protects works of art. Under certain circumstances the criteria of both laws can be met enabling the artist/designer to obtain double protection for his work. As the period of protection provided by both laws varies considerably in length (copyright: 70 years after death, registered designs: 3–15 years) this can be of notable advantage to the designer.

1.4.1 Registered designs law

Although MacKintosh chairs can be viewed in museums, most aesthetic designs for industrial products cannot be considered works of art within the meaning of the Copyright Law. It is therefore essential to register such designs according to the provisions of the Registered Designs Law in order to obtain protection from imitations. Once a design has been registered, the designer can take legal action against an infringement of his registered right.

1.4.2 Requirements for registration

The following requirements must be fulfilled for registration:

Patterns

These are two-dimensional designs, such as textiles, wall-paper prints, decoration patterns for tiles and floors.

Models

These are three-dimensional designs such as jewellery, bags, cutlery, furniture, lamps and bodywork forms for cars.

The German courts have allowed registration of any new idea that gives a finished product a special aesthetic effect or a certain tasteful idiosyncrasy. For example, this has been held to include a phosphorescent shoelace.

Novelty

Although the Registered Designs Law does not require the novelty of the pattern as a condition for registration, German courts see novelty as an implied requirement for every registration. A design that is already known in domestic specialist circles is deemed to lack novelty.

Originality

The design must also be 'original'. This requirement is similar to the inventive merit that is needed to obtain a patent. A design is seen as original, if it goes beyond average conventional work. One could say that, to be original, it must come as a surprise to the market.

1.4.3 Registration procedure

Designs are registered with the Berlin branch of the Patent Office. The following procedural requirements have to be observed to have a product entered in the designs register:

Written application

The application has to include a graphic representation of the design (photograph or drawing).

Collective application

To make the procedure more effective, there is a provision for a collective application, which can contain up to 50 different models and patterns.

Deadline

The application has to be made within six months after the first presentation of a new design at a trade fair.

Fee

The application fee is DM 100 (1991).

1.4.4 Appeals and Other Remedies

Normally, a formally correct application will lead to an entry in the Designs Register. Full legal protection of the design will result.

Every new entry in the register is published in the *Designs Gazette*. This enables competing designers to lodge an appeal to the Patent Court against false registrations. In the resulting legal proceedings the registration of the design can be withdrawn if it is shown to the satisfaction of the Court that the design lacks creative originality or novelty.

1.4.5 Scope of Protection

A registered design enjoys legal protection for a period of three years. This period can be prolonged to up to 15 years upon application.

A violator of a registered design can be sued for damages and forbearance. The burden of proving the exact amount of profits lost due to a violation of a registered design is alleviated by Art 14(*a*) of the Registered Designs Law, which allows the claimant to demand payment of the net profits made by the violator instead of damages.

1.5 Copyrights

1.5.1 Copyright Law

The Copyright Law provides a two-fold protection for intellectual property with an artistic value. Firstly, it seeks to protect what are known as the personality rights of an artist. Secondly, it deals with the commercial uses of works of art, the so-called rights of exploitation.

1.5.2 Characteristics of a Copyright

A copyright arises whenever a person creates a work of art. There is no need for a formal registration. Therefore, it is essential to provide a clear definition of what exactly can be protected by a copyright. The Copyright Law gives a definition of a work of art in its second Article: 'Works of art within the meaning of the Copyright Law are only personal, intellectual creations'.

The abstract criteria for a copyright are:

Creation of intellectual content

The work must have been a result of the use of human artistic talent and intellect.

Individuality

It must express the individual spirit of the artist. This individual, intellectual content makes a work of art distinct from unprotected mass-produced everyday work. Thus, machines and computers cannot conceive a work of art.

Creative merit

Creative forms which are very similar to previous forms do not constitute creative work. They are mere repetitions. The difficult borderline between a creation and a repetition is drawn by applying a test of similarity. In this test the court weighs the overall impression of a creation when compared with previous work. Something must strike the court as new, as above average. This point has recently become relevant for low-key creations with a minimal creative merit such as catalogues, price lists and telephone directories. The Federal Court of Justice has shown a tendency to exclude these items from protection. They are no longer viewed as containing enough creative originality to deserve copyright protection.

German copyright law recognises four categories of protected creations:

Spoken works of art

These are defined as all works which are expressed in language such as novels, diaries and poems. Problematic areas include advertising slogans and data processing programs.

Graphic art

This is defined as all works expressed by drawing and design including paintings and sculptures. As extraordinary artistic merit is required, courts tend to refuse protection to utility objects and fashion drawings, unless they are of an outstanding quality.

Photographic works and films

This category includes all work which requires the use of a camera (photographs, films and videos). Areas of dispute arise with normal photography and reporting which lacks creative merit.

Scientific work

This encompasses works of a scientific and technical nature such as drawings, maps, plans and schemes, although the borderline between these and full inventions which may be patented is often unclear. Translations and other independent creations based on existing material can also be protected.

1.5.3 PROTECTION OFFERED BY COPYRIGHT LAW

As mentioned above, the Copyright Law protects the creator's personality right and his exploitation right. It does so through civil and criminal protection.

Personality rights

The German constitution has a high regard for every individual's right to express his personality (Arts 1 and 2 of the Constitution). For this reason the German Copyright Law contains an extensive number of rights that serve to protect the artist's personality as expressed in his work of art.

These include:

(1) The Right of Publication, which is the right to decide whether or not a work is published.
(2) The Right of Creative Honour, which constitutes a ban on unauthorised amendments to a work.
(3) The Right of Acknowledgement, which is the right to be named as the creator of a work of art.

Basically all rights serve to ensure that a work of art is made accessible to the artist's contemporaries and their successors in its unamended individual form. A copyright protects a piece of art for 70 years after the death of the artist. Therefore an art collector who has purchased a painting may not add anything to the original design or remove the artists' signature from the canvas.

Right of exploitation

A second group of rules and regulations deals with the commercial value of a work of art. German law recognises the following types of exploitation:

(1) Physical forms of exploitation, including reproduction, distribution or presentation to the public of a work of art.
(2) Non-physical forms of exploitation, such as a recital, radio or television transmission or other performance of a work of art.

These actions are also covered by an additional general right of exploitation.

Other rights

Additionally the Copyright Law grants the artist a number of supplementary rights that serve to help him secure his legal position. These are:

(1) The right of access to a work, including the right to inspect, copy or reproduce the work.
(2) The right to participate in sales revenues, such as a painter's right to share in the profits of reselling a painting.
(3) The right to royalties, such as exhibition fees for works of art.

Protection against violation

The holder of a copyright has an action for forbearance and compensation against illegal violation of any of his rights mentioned above. Rather than claiming unliquidated damages such as loss of profits, which may be difficult to establish, he can demand that the violator hand over his net profit or pay a reasonable licence fee. The artist may sue for damages for loss of reputation and can further demand that all illegal copies of his work of art be destroyed.

The main difficulty a lawyer has to face when handling a claim for copyright violation is to establish clearly that the copyright has, in fact, been violated by the actions of the defendant. This is only the case if characteristic original parts of a work of art have been copied. The decision ultimately depends on an overall comparison of the protected work with the copy. The Patent Courts have a wide discretion to determine this point according to their judgment.

1.5.4 RESTRICTIONS AND EXPIRY

The copyright expires 70 years after the death of the artist. Because of its long duration, certain forms of reproducing a work of art have been exempted from copyright protection. This exemption serves to protect private and public interest in taking single copies of a work of art. The main exemptions are:

(1) individual reproduction for private use;
(2) individual reproduction for scientific research purposes (this does not apply to works of music, videos and data processing);
(3) individual productions for commercial purposes (the author can claim a reasonable fee for picture and sound recordings from the manufacturer of recording equipment (equipment fee) and from the producer of recording carriers (cassette or operator fee));
(4) reproductions and news programmes (the copies must be destroyed once the information of the general public on the work of art has been completed);
(5) public speeches on subjects which are of public interest are never protected by a copyright, although there is a duty to quote the original source of the speech.

1.5.5 TRANSFER OF COPYRIGHT

The copyright is a personality right and accordingly cannot be sold. In spite of this theoretical basis, German law recognises the fact that copyrights have a merchantable value. Thus, the artist may grant a third party the right to exploit his work. In practice two typical methods for the exploitation for a copyright have been developed:

(1) The artist or author can grant a third party certain exploitation rights for that person's use.
(2) On the other hand the author can pass his work on to another person who will exploit the work on the author's behalf.

Publishing contract

The publishing contract is a frequent example of the full transfer of exploitation rights into the hands of another person. The author passes his work to the publisher and gives him permission to reproduce and distribute the work. The author himself must abstain from exploiting his work throughout the duration of the publishing contract. In return, the publisher is under an obligation to pay the author the agreed remuneration, which will usually be a percentage of the overall sales revenue of the publication. A special publishing law exists which regulates the relationship between author and publisher in further detail.

Exploitation societies

The second customary way to make profits through the use of one's own copyright is to join an authors' society. Authors' societies safeguard the copyright of their members according to a structure that is comparable to a trust. Any author can request to be granted membership, in return for which he must grant the society use of his exploitation rights. This enables the society to pass such rights on to interested parties that wish to make use of the works of art and collect licence fees from them. Part of the fees collected will be redistributed to the members according to a special schedule.

Anybody who shows a reasonable interest in the commercial use of a copyright entered with an author's society must, on request, be granted a licence by that society. This rule serves to ensure that authors' societies cannot abuse the monopolies they often have.

The GEMA

Germany's most famous authors' society is called the GEMA. Its members are composers of works of music, who transfer all reproduction and performance rights concerning their work to the GEMA. Anybody who intends to make use of a particular musical composition which is registered with (and owned by) the GEMA must obtain the Society's permission to perform it and in return pay a tariff fee. If he fails to comply with this scheme, the GEMA will not hesitate to take legal action for violation of copyright. Through this system the GEMA has become an increasingly powerful force in the field of musical copyright in Germany. A special law dealing with the activities of exploitation societies, the Authors' Societies Law, has been introduced to control the power of such societies, which are now under the control of the Patent Office.

1.6 PROTECTION OF NAMES, LABELS AND TRADEMARKS

A third group of laws deals with the protection of company names, labels and trademarks. A full range of protective rights is provided for registered trademarks, which are governed by the Trademark Law. Additionally, there is a wide range of individual provisions contained in more general legal codes, which can serve to protect a brand name as well.

These provisions are:

(1) Article 12 of the Civil Code: Right of Name.
(2) Article 823 of the Civil Code: Protection of Personality Rights.
(3) Articles 16 and 17 of the Unfair Competition Law: Protection of Business Names and Business Secrets.
(4) Article 17 of the Commercial Code: Protection of Registered Trading Names.

Some of these rights will give an action for damages, others will only give an action for forbearance. They will be explained in more detail at the end of this chapter.

The most important protection for names and trademarks is provided by the Trademark Law (*Warenzeichengesetz* – WZG). In Germany there are more than 400,000 registered trademarks.

1.6.1 DEFINITION OF A TRADEMARK

The trademark serves to individualise a product. It is also known as a brand or brand name. To qualify for registration as a trademark, a sign or logo has to fulfil the following conditions.

Visible to the eye

A trademark has to be visible to the eye. A smell or taste cannot be registered as trademark. The most commonly encountered type of trademark is the word trademark ('Nivea', 'Persil', 'BMW'). Short phrases or sentences can also be trademarks ('The Body Shop'). Another important role is played by symbolic trademarks, such as the drawing of a little penguin as used by Penguin Books. A combination of both elements is possible as well, where a name appears using gothic or italic type or coloured letters.

Intention to use as an identifier for goods

The purpose of the trademark must be to identify goods and to contrast them with similar products of another company. This purpose need not be put into practice immediately. It is therefore possible to register a trademark and keep it in reserve for future use. Such trademarks are known as 'stored trademarks'.

Defensive trademarks

Stored trademarks must not be confused with the so-called 'defensive trademark'. Defensive trademarks aim to protect a trademark which is already in use against the dilution of its impact on the market by similar logos. A wave of registrations of defensive trademarks has confused the Trademarks Registry considerably. Therefore a new law has been enacted, which provides for a trademark to be deleted, if it has not been used for five years. The most notable weakness of defensive trademarks results from the fact that an action for violation cannot be based on them after five years have elapsed.

Description of origin

Geographic names like 'Dundee cake' or 'Dortmunder Union' can be trademarks if they are associated with products rather than simply with geographic areas, although the court practice is very restrictive in this respect.

Free trademarks

A free trademark is a word or symbol which is widely used in a particular trade without bearing a direct reference to a particular firm's product (for example, a skull to denote poison). Free trademarks cannot be registered because they are not associated with an individual product. Registration will only be effected if the applicant can show that he has managed to convert a free trademark into a symbol for his own product.

Collective trademarks

An association which consists of various independent businesses can register a collective trademark. Known examples are private wine seals or quality standards.

Packaging and get-up

The special packaging or presentation of a product, also known as get-up, cannot be registered as a trademark. It is protected by WZG, Art 22.

1.6.2 PRIORITY RULE

The same trademark must not be used for two similar products. Therefore the owner of the older trademark can claim priority, if a risk of confusion exists. The definition of a risk of confusion is one of the most difficult areas of German trademark law. Two tests have to be applied: the first test establishes the degree of similarity with regard to the competing products (test 1). If a certain degree of similarity is established, the second test is used to clarify whether or not the conflicting trademarks are similar and cause a risk of confusion (test 2).

Similarity of products (test 1)

Any goods which are interchangeable (substitute goods), are similar such as butter and margarine or sugar and sweetener. Also, goods that have a common technical purpose are regarded as being similar (shoes and rubber heels, bicycle seats and bicycles valves). There may also be a similarity between goods and services, such as a pizza delivery outlet and a pizza restaurant. There is a large grey area in which the ultimate decision depends on the circumstances of the individual case.

Similarity of symbols (test 2)

Once the similarity of the two products has been established the trademarks used for them have to be compared. The first factor is the strength of a trademark. A 'strong' trademark enjoys virtually universal market acceptance, such as BMW, whereas a weak trademark will only be known regionally. A strong trademark takes priority over a weak one and can therefore obtain universal protection—for example, the use of the trademark 'BMW' for a bicycle could conceivably lead the public to believe that BMW manufacture bicycles.

The second factor that has to be considered is the likeness to the eye and ear, as in 'ellesse' or 'bell-esse'. The overall impression of the trademark on the average consumer is decisive in such cases.

1.6.3 Registration Procedure

The following procedural requirements for registration of a trademark have to be met:

(1) A written application must be submitted on a prescribed form which can be obtained from the Patent Office.

(2) A clear pictorial representation of the trademark must be supplied.

(3) A list of the goods or services for which the trademark is to be used needs to be itemised.
(4) Payment of a registration fee of DM 300 must be made.
(5) A fee for classification of the goods (DM 60–120) must be paid.

Once the application has been received, the office will register the logo if all formal requirements have been met. Every new registration is published in the *Trademark Gazette*, which should be studied carefully to discover potentially conflicting new entries.

1.6.4 OBJECTION PROCEDURE AND OTHER REMEDIES

The office will only check a new trademark if objections have been raised. An objection fee has to be paid and a three-month deadline for objections has to be observed. Appeals on points of fact or law are possible against all decisions of the Patent Office. Further appeals on points of law may be admitted in special cases.

1.6.5 SCOPE OF PROTECTION

The holder of a trademark can prohibit any other person from using the same trademark for individual goods or services or from advertising such goods publicly.

There is an action for compensation against the violator. A malicious violation can also lead to criminal prosecution.

The protection of a trademark can be prolonged every ten years for a further ten-year period. Thus, it can last indefinitely unless the owner of the trademark fails to pay the extension fee.

1.6.6 GOODWILL PROTECTION

The German commercial and civil codes provide supplementary ways of protecting company names and goodwill.

Article 12 BGB: Right of name

Article 12 of the Civil Code protects personal names against imitation or abuse. Names of companies and clubs are included in the scope of protection as well as name-like slogans and invented names ('Hotel Forest View'). Article 12 gives the bearer of the name an action for discontinuance of the unauthorised use, although damages cannot be claimed.

Article 17 of the Commercial Code

Article 17 of the German Commercial Code protects trading names of commercial companies. Every merchant can have his trading name registered in the Commerical Registry. A trading name usually refers to the nature of a particular business (see Chapter 4 below) but it must not be misleading. Objections can be raised against a trading name which gives rise to confusion, for example, if the local greengrocer calls himself 'vegetable importer/exporter'. Furthermore, a merchant can protect his trading name against conflicting entries, although again damages cannot be claimed.

Article 823 of the Civil Code

Article 823, a provision from the law of tort, gives an action for damages if the right of name or a registered intellectual property right has been violated negligently. Thus the provision supplements the specialised laws which have been examined above because it provides an action against malicious violation that has been committed for non-commercial purposes. Thus BMW were awarded damages under Art 823 in a spectacular case featuring the use of the letters 'B', 'M', 'W' as part of an offensive joke.

Articles 16 and 17 UWG

Articles 16 and 17 of the UWG protect company names and business secrets.

Company names. Company names can play an important role in a consumer's decision to purchase a product. A good name stands for integrity and reliability. Article 16 of the UWG gives an action to protect such a name against unauthorised use by third parties. The risk of confusion for the consumer is sufficient to win the action.

Business secrets. Business secrets are all special production systems, designs and other schemes which are not otherwise protected (eg, secret recipes such as 'Pimms No 1'). Article 17 of the UWG protects such secrets against unauthorised disclosure. Both betrayal of such secrets by employees and industrial spying are criminal offences. Additionally damages can be claimed according to Art 823, Rule 2 of the Civil Code.

2
COMPETITION LAW

2.1 INTRODUCTION

Unlike most European countries which have simply enacted EEC competition law, the Federal Republic of Germany has always had its own well-developed system of national competition law. Competition law in Germany encompasses two areas, namely the law prohibiting restraints on competition (GWB) and the law against unfair competition (UWG). A first such law, prohibiting unfair advertising techniques, was enacted as early as 1904. A sequence of laws dealing with restraints on competition was enacted after the end of World War II in connection with a decartelisation initiative launched by the Allied forces. Both laws supplement each other in protecting the market from restrictions. They do so from different angles and through the application of different legal tools.

The UWG deals with the protection of the individual, company and/or consumer against unfair competition by prohibiting false advertising, commercial slander or the betraying of company secrets. The enforcement of the UWG depends on the initiative of the individual, company or consumer protection society who have to bring an action against unfair competition to protect their position.

The GWB covers those restraints on competition, which are perceived to endanger the free market economy, and therefore protects the interests of the general public. The main areas of application are preventing price cartels, controlling the merger of powerful companies or interfering with restrictive distribution systems of brand name products. The law is administered by the Federal Cartels Office in Berlin, which can prohibit agreements, dissolve trusts and impose fines.

In the field of competition law, national law overlaps with EEC law to a very large extent. This is particularly true for the

GWB, which cannot take priority over Arts 85 and 86 of the Treaty of Rome. A conflict occurs whenever restrictions of trade affect more than one EEC member state, which happens very frequently. It is therefore necessary to give a brief outline of the collision rules which apply. In the field of competition law it is generally accepted that Community Law takes priority over national law. In cases of conflict, national law is overridden so that EEC Law can be applied uniformly throughout the whole community. This has several effects:

(1) Cartels which have been permitted by the Commission cannot be prohibited by German cartels authorities. German law will only prevail if no decision by the Commission exists.
(2) Any action which is prohibited by EEC law cannot be encouraged by national law.
(3) Parallel proceedings remain possible as long as they do not lead to contradictory decisions. To avoid conflicting results, national proceedings must be stayed if European proceedings are commenced.
(4) To avoid double-punishment, a fine imposed by one authority has to be deducted from a new fine.
(5) In the case of merger permissions, German authorities are theoretically obliged to follow the guidance of the Commission. However, national authorities have shown great reluctance to give up what is perceived as a well-balanced mergers and monopolies control system and the Federal Court of Justice currently refuses to acknowledge the supremacy of EEC law in this respect.

Altogether it appears that European law has not yet developed its full impact on national competition policies. With the European single market planned for 1992 the position must, however, be expected to change.

2.2 THE LAW OF UNFAIR COMPETITION (UWG)

The UWG aims to protect individual businesses and consumers against unfair trading techniques. To achieve this purpose two types of laws and regulations have been enacted. On the one hand the UWG contains some so-called 'general rules', which are characterised by a particularly wide wording. On the other hand, individual rules have been formulated, which deal with widespread trading techniques separately. Examples of these are:

(1) General rules;
   (a) Article 1 prohibits unethical trading techniques;
   (b) Article 3 prohibits misleading advertising techniques.
(2) Individual rules;
   (a) Articles 6(a) and 6(b) regulate wholesale business;
   (b) Articles 7(d), 7(b), 7(c) and 9 regulate end of season and closing down sales;
   (c) Article 12 deals with bribery of employees;
   (d) Article 17 deals with betrayal of business secrets;
   (e) Articles 14 and 15 protect the 'goodwill' of the company.

While the individualised provisions have a clear content the interpretation of the general rules of Arts 1 and 3 is one of the most complicated problems of unfair competition law. Although precedents do not have the force of law in Germany, they constitute the main source of legal guidance when interpreting those general rules.

The Federal Court of Justice has developed various categories of cases, which fall within the scope of application of UWG, Arts 1 and 3.

Competitive situations

A general requirement for most regulations of the UWG is the existence of competition between the parties involved in the legal dispute. This requirement has virtually become obsolete because the courts have begun to interpret it in the widest possible way. It is presumed to be a fact of life that traders will normally act with a view to promoting their own business in order to gain an advantage over competitors. Thus in the *Dimple* decision the Federal Court of Justice decided that a competitive situation can exist between a manufacturer of whisky and a manufacturer of cosmetic articles.

2.2.1 ARTICLE 1

Article 1 of the UWG is usually applied to disputes involving five different categories of unethical trading techniques,

which are:
(1) Unethical poaching of customers.
(2) Imposing unfair hindrances on competitors.
(3) Unfair exploitation of another person's achievements.
(4) Unfair disturbance of the balance of the market.
(5) Any breach of law.

In the following paragraphs, these categories shall be examined in further detail.

Unethical poaching of customers ('passing off')

A company which enters the market with a product or service will need to recruit its first customers from the clientele of other firms. It may of course do so as long as it observes the rules of fairness and respects the customers' freedom of choice. If it breaks those rules it is engaged in prohibited customer poaching, which can be done in various ways:

(1) Misleading statements: it is prohibited to poach a customer through untrue or discouraging advertisements.
(2) Pressurising: it is prohibited to exert physical or psychological pressure on customers, such as by a targeted approach to passers-by on public roads or unrequested telephone calls.
(3) Value advertising and gifts: promising good value prices or gifts to customers can be considered unfair, if it puts moral pressure on them to make a purchase. For example, offering 'free radio if you purchase £50 worth of goods now'.
(4) Exploitation of feelings: false appeals to charity, helpfulness or generosity are prohibited, such as pretending that goods have been made by blind or handicapped people.

It must be emphasised that there are further, less prominent, examples of customers poaching not listed above.

Imposing unfair hindrance

Rather than poaching customers, a newcomer on the market could be tempted to hinder his competitors in their business success. Hindrance includes all hostile attacks that are directed against the person of a competitor or his company, eg, boycott or defamation.

Exploitation of someone else's achievements

It might appear attractive to imitate the successful trading concept or product of another company, but this is obviously illegal if the competing company holds a patent for that product or concept. Unprotected business ideas such as pizza delivery, may principally be imitated. However, UWG, Art 1 limits the ways and means of such imitation. Thus systematic and slavish copying is considered to be an act of unfair competition.

Headhunting

Headhunting is prohibited, if it is done by means of misleading information or by promising inappropriate benefits. Even if no such means are employed, German courts tend to disapprove of headhunting, as it is seen as enticement to commit a breach of contract.

Breach of law

It may occasionally appear profitable to disregard statutory rules governing production of goods or working conditions in order to be able to produce goods more cheaply than other competitors. This is a case of unfair competition through breach of law.

Market disturbance

Any attempt to establish a monopoly in a particular market is viewed very unfavourably by German law. Therefore, the UWG prohibits unfair means of developing a strong market position, such as agressive price undercutting.

2.2.2 ARTICLE 3

A second general rule of eminent importance for questions of unfair trade is UWG, Art 3, which deals with advertising techniques. Again different groups of cases can be distinguished:

(1) Deceit concerning the characteristics of a company.
(2) Superlative advertising.
(3) Deceit concerning the purpose of a sale.
(4) Price deception.
(5) Deceit concerning goods and services.

A central committee issues general guidelines and recommendations on fair advertising, but their observance cannot be enforced. They will, however, be admissible evidence in an advertising dispute. The following section will deal with the most frequent cases of unfair advertising.

Misleading statements made for competition purposes

The general rule stated by UWG, Art 3 is that all misleading statements which are made for competition purposes are prohibited.

The term statement includes all presentations of fact, including price, descriptive text or imaginative symbol. Opinions can also contain a statement, as can sound, for example, the noise of clucking hens used in a radio advert for egg pastries is misleading, if the pastries are made with dried egg.

Anything which can be misunderstood by the average consumer is misleading. A true statement can mislead the consumer if it contains ambiguous language. The question is judged from the point of view of the customer, whose impression is determined by market researches. German courts tend to assume that the average consumer does not view an advertisement critically. It is usually sufficient that a considerable group of consumers misunderstand the statements (usually 10 to 15 per cent, sometimes as little as 5 to 6 per cent).

Accordingly, advertising standards have become rather strict in Germany, when compared with other European countries.

Deceit

Unfair advertising is characterised by deception which influences the purchasing decision of the consumer.

The goodwill of the company is a major decision making factor for the average consumer, who often prefers to purchase goods at a higher price, because they are produced by a well-known company. Therefore it is deceitful to describe falsely:

(1) The size and age of a company.
(2) The title and name of its owner.
(3) The turnover or circulation numbers.
(4) The workforce or circulation figures of a company.

Deceit can also occur concerning goods and services. The temptation to describe or represent one's goods or services too favourably in order to influence the consumer's purchasing decision is undoubtedly great. This can be done by:

(1) Using substitute low quality goods.
(2) Making misrepresentations about the origin of goods (eg, 'handmade').
(3) False geographical statements which are linked with quality expectations (eg, 'Persian rug' or 'Scotch whisky').
(4) Quantity lies such as giving an inaccurate weight.

(5) False representations about the source of a purchase (eg, 'ex factory').

Medical advertising

Advertisements concerning medical products are subject to additional restrictions which are prescribed by a special law on medical advertising. Such adverts must be free from any emotional appeals to the consumer. It is considered particularly unethical to use stories of miraculous recovery or clinical pictures in medical advertising. Creating false fears and worries about health is also prohibited.

Price deception

The main factor in most purchasing decisions still remains the price of a product, with the consumer wanting to feel that he got good value for his money. Because of the frequency of pricing offences, the German Parliament has introduced a pricing ordinance. The following rules for correct pricing apply:

(1) Price clarity: price labels must be easily legible and specify the correct end price (inclusive of VAT). Complicated discounts based on percentage calculations or difficult sums are not permitted.

(2) Price slogans: price slogans, especially the ones indicating exceptionally low prices, must be true and unambiguous,eg, 'discount price', 'wholesale price'.

(3) Price comparisons: price comparisons of every kind are prohibited in Germany. This includes advertising, which compares former prices of a product with new discount or sales prices, as well as advertisements which contrast the prices of two different companies (eg, 'WAS DM 100, NOW DM 39.95').

(4) Sales under cost price: special offers and under cost sales are prohibited, if they are designed to create a false impression of the price-level of the entire range of products. The advertisement must therefore denote the quantity of goods available at the cut price (eg, 'two only', 'limited quantities' or 'one only per customer').

Deception concerning the purpose of a sale

Consumers are often lured into purchasing unwanted and unneeded items through the announcements of end of season sales, clearance sales or closing down sales. To protect consumers and competitors, the UWG prohibits misrepresentations about the purpose of the sale. Furthermore, closing down sales or anniversary sales are only permitted on a restricted scale. They have to be announced to the local administration, which will ensure that a closing down sale is not followed by the immediate reopening of the same business on the same premises.

Superlative advertising

Another widespread method of deceitful advertising is describing a product or a business as leading in its field or as superior to ordinary goods and products (eg, 'the best kitchen machine', 'Europe's biggest furniture shop').

Advertising slogans of this kind must not arouse false expectations in the customers. If one wishes to use a superlative in advertising, it is therefore important to word the slogan very carefully to make sure that it tells the truth. A product which is described as 'top quality German product' must be in the leading group of quality goods of its kind in Germany. Many firms have therefore resorted to using simplified purchase appeals which do not contain a definite core of facts because such slogans do not amount to superlative advertising (eg, 'AEG Lawamat, that and no other', 'Mummy always gives us the best').

2.2.3 IMPACT OF THE EUROPEAN ADVERTISING DIRECTIVE ON GERMAN LAW (DIRECTIVE 84/450)

German law is generally in harmony with the European advertising directive. The range of protection provided by German law sometimes even goes beyond that offered by the Directive. Examples of this are the strict prohibition of comparative advertising and price comparisons demanded by German law and the definition of the average consumer as being uncritical by German courts.

This discrepancy does not invalidate the German law, because the current harmonisation programme launched by the European Commission aims to protect the consumer and does not hinder overprotection. Thus German UWG and EEC law stand side by side.

2.2.4 Courses of action arising out of unfair competition law

Unfair trading techniques can lead to compensation claims and claims for discontinuance. A claim for discontinuance can be brought by an individual competitor or by a consumer protection society or trader's association. Societies and associations can only bring claims for discontinuance, with damages only being awarded to individual competitors. It is not clear if a consumer, who has been deceived by a misleading advertisement, also has a claim for damages under the UWG. Recent claims by disappointed customers have usually been unsuccessful.

2.2.5 Procedural peculiarities

Certain procedural peculiarities have developed for the settlement of unfair trading disputes in Germany. Rather than bringing a legal action before a court of law the injured party or consumer society issues so-called 'warnings', in which they demand that the violator promise that he will abstain in future from employing a particular trading technique which is alleged to be unfair. If the violator refuses to make a statement to this effect, an application for a temporary injunction is made to the court. Temporary injunctions are dealt with immediately and result in the issuance of a temporary order against the violator. The application for an injunction needs to emphasise the urgency of the matter. Full evidence need not be given and the court will usually decide without an oral hearing. Therefore, it has become practice for the other side to submit a *caveat* which serves as an informal defence against the application for an injunction. The court is obliged to take the contents of the *caveat* into consideration before deciding the dispute.

Because of this peculiar practice unfair advertising disputes and similar matters are usually settled after the decision about the injunction has been made by the court.

2.3 Cartels, monopolies and mergers

The German law prohibiting restraints on competition (GWB) is based on a concept which is very similar to that of

American anti-trust law. Furthermore, European competition law greatly influences and overlaps the national legislation. The use of Arts 85 and 86 of the EEC Treaty will therefore be dealt with in the relevant paragraphs.

The GWB encompasses three main fields of restraints on competition:

(1) The control of cartels or horizontal contracts, which usually take the form of a price cartel and involve several commercial enterprises which operate on the same market level.

(2) The supervision of vertical contracts which have the effect of restricting trade, such as distribution agreements between a manufacturer and his retailers.

(3) The control of mergers and acquisitions (or fusions).

A very important fourth element, the 'decartelisation' (dissolving of existing trusts), has not yet been approached by Parliament. With problems of reunification taking priority for the foreseeable future, the introduction of a decartelisation regulation will unfortunately be delayed for some more time.

2.3.1 AUTHORITIES

German competition law is implemented almost exclusively by the Federal Cartels Office in Berlin. This Office enjoys a fair degree of independence from the Government, although it is a federal authority. Local cartels offices supplement the activities of the Cartels Office in Berlin.

Reports and influential recommendations on fusion control are given by the Monopolies Commission in Cologne. The recommendations of this Commission have become a powerful factor in the application of German competition law.

2.3.2 PROCEDURES

Decisions of the German cartels authorities are reached according to a formalised procedure, which in many respects resembles court procedure.

Preliminary investigation

A formal investigation of a case is usually preceded by a preliminary investigation which will lead to an inspection of documents and discussions with the firms involved. Often such discussions lead to changes in a contract that are acceptable to all sides. In this event the cartels office will refrain from interference.

Formal procedure

If the preliminary procedure does not lead to satisfactory results, the cartels office will automatically commence a formal procedure. During this phase oral hearings with solicitors will take place and evidence will be admitted. Once the hearing has been closed, a formal decision will be issued. Injunctions can be issued which enforce a decision of the cartels office and disobedient parties can be fined.

Appeals against final decisions of a cartel's authority can be made to the regional Court of Appeal (*Oberlandesgericht*). Most appeals are dealt with by the Chamber Court in Berlin, because the Federal Cartels Office is situated there.

Actions for injured parties

Parties which have suffered from the prohibited activities of cartels, or other agreements in restriction of trade, have an action for compensation under the Cartels Law. Since the amount of damages is often very difficult to establish, this right has only gained marginal importance. A more powerful tool against cartels is a protective injunction, which can also be implemented as a preventive injunction against future violations. Finally, issues of cartels law can be used as a defence in commercial litigation, when members of a cartel or other dominant market forces seek to enforce an agreement which restricts trade. The defendant can plead that such agreements are void and therefore unenforceable.

2.4 THE CONTENTS OF GERMAN CARTELS LAW

The GWB divides agreements in restriction of trade into the categories of horizontal and vertical agreements.

Horizontal agreements in restriction of trade are:

- Prohibited cartels.
- Licensed cartels.
- Registered cartels.
- Opposed cartels.

Vertical agreements in restriction of trade are:

- Vertical price ties.
- Distribution systems.

- Exclusivity ties and package deals.
- Licensing contracts.
- Restrictions on the use of goods.

Parties to a horizontal agreement or cartel act on the same market level (there being three main market levels which are: production, wholesale, and retail). Parties to a vertical agreement act on different market levels (eg, a contract between a producer of goods and a wholesale business).

2.4.1 THE DEFINITION OF A CARTEL

Cartels are defined as contracts between companies which can lead to manipulation of the free market forces through restriction of competition. The scope of application of this definition has constantly been enlarged by the German courts. Every phrase used has been given a specific meaning through judicial precedent.

Company

Most rules and regulations of the GWB only apply to 'companies'. Any person or organisation who pursues an independent commercial purpose involving production or distribution of goods or services can be deemed a 'company'. This includes non-profit making societies, self-employed entrepreneurs and clubs.

The main legal problem concerning the word 'company' is the question of whether or not it includes conglomerates of companies. If a contract has been concluded between related mother and daughter companies of the same group, they can be viewed as one commercial unit and, as a result, no cartel can be formed. However, some groups are only loosely connected, leaving all member companies room to compete against each other. In such cases a cartel can conceivably be formed.

Exempted companies

Strong lobbying took place when the current competition law was about to be enacted by Parliament. The following commercial interest groups succeeded in gaining exemptions from the cartel ban:

(1) Transport industries (airlines, mail, railways).
(2) Agriculture.
(3) Banking and insurance concerns.

(4) Coal and steel industries.
(5) Power, gas and water industries.

However, except for transport and agriculture these industries are subject to European competition law, where they do not enjoy a privileged treatment. Up to now the commission has been rather generous with the implementation of EEC law in these politically delicate areas. Moves appear to be afoot to tighten the practice in this respect, but no new rules and regulations have yet been passed.

Contract

A 'contract' is required between the companies that form a cartel. The word 'contract' has to be considered in conjunction with Art 25, s 1 of the GWB, which includes 'agreed activities' in the cartel prohibition. The words 'agreed activities' are obviously much broader in meaning than the word 'contract'. As a result, all of the following agreements may constitute a prohibited cartel:

- A genuine contract.
- A non-enforceable contract.
- A gentlemens' agreement.
- Coordinated activities.
- Joint recommendations.

The major legal problem that arises is how to distinguish prohibited coordinated activities from mere parallel action. Basically, this question is one of evidence, as clear proof of coordinated activity is rarely found. Therefore, the courts look at the risks connected with normal autonomous action and ask whether those risks are eliminated by coordinated action. In an oligopolistic market, it is very difficult to establish whether a price rise results from coordination, or from the fact that all companies follow the lead of a 'price pioneer'. A good example of this process is the petrol market, in which a price-war never appears to emerge. Another example of prohibited coordination is the creation of mutual information systems.

Manipulation of the market

A cartel contract must lead to a noticeable manipulation of the market. The difficulty that one encounters with this phrase is how to define the area of commerce which constitutes 'the market' — there being no all-encompassing universal market in an economic system. On the contrary, a market economy is made up by numerous different markets and sub-markets (thus the market for cars consists of sub-markets for, say, luxury cars, family cars, and small cars). The limits of such markets are defined by the concept of functional interchangeability. This means that all goods which are interchangeable in the eyes of the average consumer are included in a particular market. Furthermore, territorial factors and transport costs must be taken into consideration. Therefore, local, regional, national and international markets exist. Thus, an agreement between the owners of the only two toy shops on a remote island to double-charge for toys at Christmas can be a cartel, because it manipulates the local toy market.

Restriction of competition

Artificial limitations on the free play of the market forces are generally held to be unwelcome. The commercial freedom to act according to one's own marketing concept must therefore not be restricted. Commercial freedom and its restrictions are measured in so-called parameters. The main market parameters are:

- Price.
- Price components.
- Quantity.
- Territory of distribution.
- Terms and conditions of sale.
- Credit and investment power.

If these parameters are manipulated competition has been restricted.

Intention

The question of whether the restriction on competitions has to be intentional is disputed in Germany. Difficulties arise in the case of pools for the purpose of purchasing or selling goods. The main purpose of such pools is to save costs for all members and to improve their bargaining position. A side effect of a pool may, however, be a price coordination. As it cannot always be proved that such side effects were intended, a strong body of opinion favours the inclusion of unintentional restrictions into the definition of a cartel.

Cartels in European law

The basic concepts of German and European cartel law are very similar. The main differences arise from the fact that EEC law is aimed at the protection of a European market economy characterised by the free circulation of goods throughout the Community. According to Art 85 of the Treaty of Rome a cartel encompasses '. . all measures which are designed to impair trade between member states . .'. Both the European Court of Justice and the Commission have given this community market clause a very wide scope of application. It has been read to include contracts between national companies, if such contracts indirectly affect the realisation of a uniform European market. The other characteristics of a European cartel are interpreted similarly to German law.

One more point is worthy of mention. The European Commission takes a stricter view than German courts on the formation of joint ventures, which can lead to a wide range of coordination of activity through the so-called 'group effect'. Rather than competing in the market covered by the joint venture, the parent companies will usually withdraw from that market. The Commission is therefore inclined to prohibit joint ventures which would be permissable under German law.

2.4.2 PRIVILEGED CARTELS

Although the formation of a cartel is prohibited in principle, German law allows for numerous exemptions from this rule. Cartels can either be legalised by mere registration or by obtaining express cartel permission. Some registrations can also be opposed by the cartels authorities.

Exempted Groups

The following groups of exempted cartels exist:

(1) Mere registration cartels, which can take the form of cartels agreeing on standards or shapes of products or rationalisation cartels, must only be registered with the Cartels Authority to escape the general ban.

(2) Some registration cartels can be opposed by the Cartels Authority, such as specialisation cartels or discount cartels. They are banned as soon as they are notified of the opposition.

(3) Other cartels can be permitted under a Minister license, such as a structural crisis cartel, or under a Cartels Authority license, in the case of an export or import cartel.

To obtain exemption, it is essential that all parties involved notify the Federal Cartels Office of the formation of a cartel as soon as possible. Without notification a cartel is always prohibited and the cartel contract will be null and void.

Notification

The notification needs to contain detailed information on the structure of the cartel. The main points that need to be disclosed are:

(1) Name and address of all companies involved.
(2) Legal structure and address of the cartel.
(3) Naming of the official representative of the cartel.

Other details on the purposes of the cartel will have to be given in order to avoid a rejection of the notification by the Cartels Office on the grounds that it is not eligible for exemption.

European law: block exemptions

One of the main differences between German and European cartel law is to be found in the nature of the exemption system. The European system of exemption is based on Art 85, s 3 of the Treaty of Rome, which provides for the possibility of declaring the general cartel ban inapplicable to certain groups of contracts and resolutions known as block exemptions. Individual exemptions can also be granted and it is important to know what type of cartels are tolerated in this manner by the European Commission.

Small and medium-sized businesses will need to cooperate on a European level in order to penetrate the Common Market. Therefore, the Commission permits cooperative agreements if some of the resulting benefits are passed on to the consumer in the form of reduced prices or better distribution of goods.

Cooperative agreements which serve to promote technical progress can also be exempted from the cartel ban, always provided, however, that a reasonable degree of free competition is retained. Furthermore, the restrictions imposed on the participating companies must be essential for the achievement of the technical progress.

Most of the other exceptions to the cartel ban provided by German law do not have a corresponding group exception under Art 85, s 3. In theory, German export and import cartels are therefore prohibited. The fate of structural crisis cartels and discount or condition cartels has also become open to discussion.

No clear policy of the Commission has yet been distinguished in this area. A full synopsis of German and European Law is provided in section **2.4.4** below.

2.4.3 VERTICAL AGREEMENTS

Vertical agreements such as sales and distribution contracts can impose unwelcome restrictions on trade, such as manufacturers' price clauses seeking to establish the reselling price.

Price ties

The main example of vertical agreements is price ties. Their introduction to the market is strictly prohibited. This includes the fixing of maximum or minimum prices as well as profit margins or bans on discount prices. Only non-binding recommendations for prices of brand name articles are permitted (*unverbindliche Preisempfehlung*). The only exemption to this ban concerns books and other printed products (magazines, calendars), which are traditionally sold in book shops. Contractual clauses which seek to violate the general ban on price ties are null and void and therefore unenforceable. Furthermore, the violator can be fined very heavily by the cartel authorities.

Exclusivity ties

In contrast to price ties, other vertical restrictions which seek to establish exclusive use of contractual terms and conditions are not automatically void. Instead, they are subject to supervision by the cartel authorities which can declare them null and void if they impose unfair restrictions on the affected companies. This will usually be the case if they are simultaneously imposed on a large number of companies and therefore restrict market access for newcomers. An exclusivity contract must be made in writing and submitted to the Cartels Authority for inspection. The main types of such contracts are:

Restrictions of the freedom of usage. Sometimes a supplier of goods will seek to prevent his customers from combining his products with goods produced by other competitors. In the case of the *United Shoe Machinery Corporation* this was done by means of rental contracts which obliged shoe manufacturers to set up the rented machines in a certain prescribed order. Violation of this order resulted in withdrawal of the machines. Such clauses can be declared void.

Restrictions on Third Party Dealings (distribution ties). Restrictions imposed on the right of one party to purchase goods from or sell goods to certain third parties can be declared void by the Cartels Authority. This particular group of ties is of eminent practical importance for the distribution of brand name products. They are commonly encountered as selective distribution systems which confine delivery of a brand name product to specially selected traders. Each trader will usually be guaranteed a sales monopoly for his assigned area. In return he will have to limit his sales transactions to contracts with the end consumer. The best known example of selective distribution systems is featured by the car industry, which usually delivers new cars to appointed traders only. Although these systems are highly restrictive they are permitted under German law unless the Cartels Authority interferes. However, corresponding EEC law may invalidate the contract.

Restrictions on the purchase/sale of supplementary goods. Distribution systems are often accompanied by flanking provisions concerning the purchase/sale of supplementary goods such as spare parts of servicing equipment. Car manufacturers and breweries tend to demand that such goods be purchased exclusively from their own stocks. This can result in severe restrictions on the dealer's freedom of trade, which are viewed very unfavourably by both German and European cartel authorities. The recent abolishment of single beer pubs in England serves as a good example of the developments in this area.

Package deals. Sometimes the manufacturer of a successful product will seek to exploit this success for the marketing of his less popular goods. He will try to make all customers buy both the successful and the unsuccessful product in a package. This method is particularly effective if the manufacturer holds a monopoly for the successful product. Package deals are widespread in the film industry, where cinemas are often requested to purchase ten or more films consisting of perhaps three Oscar winning movies packaged with seven unpopular programmes. Under German law, such package deals can be prohibited if they lead to unfair trade restrictions. Under EEC law they are usually void.

Licensing contracts

Licensing contracts deal with the purchase or use of patented inventions, registered designs and other protective rights. Such contracts are commercially necessary and legally permitted unless they attempt to overprotect the invention concerned. Overprotection occurs whenever a licensing contract tries to expand the scope of the protective right beyond the limit prescribed by the law. Only the following items can be regulated in licensing contracts:

(1) Type, quantity, territory and length of time for the use of the protective rights.
(2) Restrictions which ensure technically correct exploitation.
(3) The price.
(4) Non-aggression clauses (duty not to seek deletion of the protective right).

European law

Other than the GWB, Art 85 of the Treaty of Rome does not make a distinction between horizontal and vertical contracts. Both powers of restrictions on competition are null and void, unless an exemption is granted for their performance. Exemptions for certain groups of vertical agreements have been granted by the European Commission (block exemptions).

Distribution systems. The Commission tends to view distribution systems and other exclusive sale contracts favourably, because they promote EEC-wide market penetration. Therefore Ordinance 67/67 contains a group exemption for certain types of exclusive distribution systems. It has to be noted, however, that restrictions on parallel imports will not be tolerated. The Commission will only maintain systems which are designed to maintain the quality standards that the public expects of a brand name product (such as well-schooled personnel, satisfactory presentation). Additional unnecessary restrictions (cross supply bans, quantative requirements) are not tolerated by the Commission unless an extraordinary need for close cooperation between the manufacturer of the product and the dealer is shown (for instance, to avoid health hazards for the customer). In most cases EEC law rather than German law should therefore be considered when questions of distribution ties arise.

Licensing. The licensing contract is another type of vertical agreement which is viewed quite favourably by the European Commission as long as the contract in question does not contain:

- Price ties.
- Purchasing restrictions.
- Overlong duration period.

The decisions of the Commission are based on the principle of exhaustion, which implies that a protective right is exhausted in all member states after it has been brought into free circulation in one member state.

2.4.4 COMPARISON TO EEC LAW

In summary, the following comparison of various cartels under German and EEC law may be made.

(1) Cartel: Principally banned under German and EEC law.
(2) Joint venture: Allowed under German law if parent companies withdraw from the market. Principally banned under EEC law.
(3) Conglomerate: Only loose conglomerates can form a cartel under German law. Conglomerates do not normally form a cartel under EEC law.
(4) Condition cartel: Allowed under German law if notified. Probably banned under EEC law.
(5) Discount cartel: Allowed if notified and not opposed under German law. Probably banned under EEC law.
(6) Structural crisis cartel: Special permission by Minister of Economics necessary under German law. Probably banned under EEC law.
(7) Cooperation cartel: Can be permitted under German law, but only for small and medium sized businesses under EEC law.
(8) Specialisation cartel: Allowed under German law if notified. Permission possible under EEC law if they promote technical progress.
(9) Export cartel: Permission possible under German law. Banned under EEC law.
(10) Import cartel: Permission possible under German law. Banned under EEC law.
(11) Price ties: Banned except for books under German law. Banned under EEC law.
(12) Distribution systems: Allowed under German law but

bannable. Partly allowed under EEC law (Ordinance 67–67).

(13) Licensing contracts: Allowed under German law. Partly allowed under EEC law.

2.5 COMPANIES WHICH DOMINATE THE MARKET

In order to stabilise and further enhance a strong market position, some companies will attempt to eliminate competitors or discriminate against them. To prevent the abuse of market power, German law provides for the Cartels Authorities to supervise companies which dominate the market. Additionally the victim has an action for equal treatment.

2.5.1 ABUSE OF MARKET POWER

German law recognises three main types of abuse of market power. These are:

(1) Hindrance abuse: imposing unfair hindrances to prevent other companies from succeeding in a market, such as cutting prices to eliminate smaller companies.

(2) Price abuse: promoting unnatural price developments and manipulating prices.

(3) Discrimination: imposing discriminatory terms and conditions on certain companies, such as refusing to deliver goods to discount stores.

When dealing with problems of abuse, the main difficulty the legal practitioner encounters is to establish the market conditions which would prevail if no 'abuse' had occurred.

The so-called comparative market concept is used to find out the correct (hypothetical) market conditions. In the case of price abuse a justification test is applied asking whether a price increase can be explained by objective changes in market conditions.

To establish a case of discrimination two actual situations are compared. The treatment of the company who is discriminated against is compared to the treatment of other companies. If there is no reasonable explanation for a difference in treatment, the dominant company acts obtrusively and equal treatment can be claimed.

2.5.2 DOMINANT POSITION ON THE MARKET

The above rights only work against dominant companies. Market dominance is assessed with respect to the structure of the market concerned. It can either occur if a market leader is not exposed to any noticeable competition or if a small group of companies divide most of the market between themselves in an oligopolic market.

The law assumes that a dominant position exists in the following cases:

(1) In an oligopolic market, which exists where a small number of companies share a large part of the market, the law assumes market dominance where four or five companies share $\frac{2}{3}$ of the market, and the annual turnover of each company exceeds DM 100,000,000.

(2) The same assumption applies where two or three companies share half the market, and the annual turnover of each exceeds DM 250,000,000.

(3) In a monopolic market, where one market leader is not exposed to any considerable competition, market dominance is assumed where a single company has $\frac{1}{3}$ of the market.

Regardless of these assumptions, market dominance can always be established in an individual case. To calculate the size of a market share the turnover of affiliated or amalgamated companies is added up. Such factors as circulation figures, number of employees, or access to resources can be taken into consideration as well.

2.5.3 EUROPEAN LAW

In contrast to German law, European law is more restrained in establishing market dominance. The Commission requires market shares of over 45 per cent to assume domination without further proof. Lower shares (20–40 per cent) need to coincide with additional factors to indicate a considerable lead over competitors. Abuse is defined along the lines of the same principles that apply in German law. The main difference that remains is that the EEC Treaty is only applicable if the affected market represents a major part of the Common Market. The territory of each member state (apart from Luxembourg) forms a large part of the Community, but smaller areas may also suffice.

2.5.4 Courses of Action

Article 26 of the GWB provides a course of action for companies which suffer from discriminative trading techniques and other forms of abuse of market power. Three types of action can be distinguished:

(1) Boycott. A complete blockade of access to supplies and other commercial sources.
(2) Discrimination against dependent small or medium-sized suppliers or buyers.
(3) Hindrance. Imposing unfair hindrances on other companies.

Extensive case law exists on incidents of discrimination. Three groups of cases of particular importance deserve some further attention.

Delivery blockades. It is often difficult to draw the borderline between a well-structured distribution organisation and delivery blockades. The mere refusal to incorporate a company into a distribution system does not amount to a blockade. It only becomes a blockade if the dominant company cannot provide a good reason for the refusal.

Demand for concessions. Sometimes the bargaining power of the parties can be reversed with the result that the buyer, rather than the supplier, makes demands for special concessions. Thus big purchasers will ask for 'counter fees' if a supplier wants his product put on a shelf in their stores. Such demands are abusive unless they are matched by genuine counter service on the part of the buyer (for example, big supermarkets often charge counter fees for putting a product on eye level shelves).

Dependent companies. If the supplier or buyer depends on contracting with a market leader because he cannot otherwise complete his range of goods, the law gives him a right to demand supplies. Thus Rossignol were ordered to continue delivery of their racing skis to a Munich Sporthaus, as the Sporthaus was deemed to be at a severe disadvantage on the market if it could not longer offer Rossignol skis to its customers.

2.6 Merger Control

In 1973 Germany enacted a tight and sophisticated system of merger control to stop the incessant advances of market concentration in the country. The amount of markets which are dominated by one or more companies has increased constantly. Therefore, merger control aims to prevent the creation of additional market domination.

2.6.1 THE SYSTEM OF FUSION CONTROL

The GWB contains a sophisticated system of definitions and legal assumptions which serve to ensure that all relevant mergers are caught in the net of fusion control.

As a first step the law sets a bottom line for the size of the companies that are to be screened. Thus if the combined turnover of the companies involved does not exceed DM 500 million, or the entire market turnover does not exceed DM 10 million, or the company which is taken over has a turnover of under DM 50 million, then the companies are free to fuse.

If a merger does not fall into these exemption categories the next step is to check whether the law assumes that the merger will lead to the creation of a dominant market provision. The following list gives the four assumptions of the creation of market dominance:

(1) Penetration of a market which is characterised by the predominance of two or more medium sized firms by large companies (ie, with a turnover of at least DM 2 billion).
(2) The merger of large companies with a turnover of at least DM 2 billion, with dominant ones.
(3) 'Elephant weddings' which are mergers of companies with a combined turnover of DM 12 billion and an individual turnover of DM 1 billion.
(4) Fusions within the leading group of an oligopoly, where three or less companies control 50 per cent of the market or five or less companies control $\frac{2}{3}$ of the market.

The companies involved in such a merger are at liberty to prove that the assumption of market dominance does not meet the truth in their particular case. They need to show that the intended fusion will improve the competition situation on their particular market. Thus, a merger might put a medium sized company in a position to reopen competition with a market leader.

As a last step, the Cartels Office can attempt to prove that an individual case of market dominance can be established, though the criteria of the assumptions have not been met. This can be the case if the intended fusion will eliminate competition on a market although the companies involved do not reach the turnover sizes described in the assumptions.

Extraordinary cases of merger can be permitted by the Minister of Economic Affairs, if the overall economic benefits of the merger outweigh its disadvantages (such as with the merger of Daimler-Benz with Messerschmidt-Bölkow-Blohm).

2.6.2 NOTIFICATION PROCEDURE

Most mergers have to be notified to the Federal Cartels Office, either before or after their completion.

Notification must occur before completion where there are two companies with a turnover of DM 1 billion involved, or where one company has a turnover of over DM 2 billion. It is sufficient to notify the Cartels Office after completion of the merger where a market share of 20 per cent or more is achieved, or where the companies involved have either at least 10,000 employees, or a turnover of DM 500 million, but do not reach the figures mentioned above.

Other mergers may be notified, if the companies involved want to find out whether they are likely to encounter any objections from the Cartels Office. Absence of a notification duty by no means hinders a merger investigation.

3
BUSINESS ORGANISATION AND COMPANY FORMATION

3.1 INTRODUCTION

German law provides for a rich diversity of business organisations. Two basic types of legal structures for the formation of a business can be distinguished; the partnership and the legal entity.

Partnerships include the following categories:

(1) General partnership (oHG).
(2) Limited partnership (KG).
(3) Silent partnership.
(4) Ship-owning partnership (*Reederei*).

Legal entities comprise the following:

(1) Limited liability company (GmbH).
(2) Public limited company (AG).
(3) Mutual insurance company (VVaG).
(4) Cooperative company (eG).

Most of these companies have to be registered in a commercial register (*Handelsregister*) which is kept at the local court (*Amtsgericht*).

A special gazette publishes all major details concerning a registered company such as its name and the name of its representatives. Companies which are legal entities commence their existence with registration, whereas partnerships and sole trading companies are legally existent as soon as they commence their business, although failure to register can result in fines.

The implementation of recent EEC publicity directives has led to another difference between legal entities on the one hand and partnerships on the other hand. While the former have to publish their accounts in great detail, partnerships are currently exempted from this obligation.

Taxation aspects may also influence the choice of a

particular company formation. Although double taxation is usually avoided by German tax law some taxes, like the wealth tax, are taxed both on the profits of the legal entity and on the profits of the shareholder.

3.2 PARTNERSHIPS AND SOLE TRADERS

Partnerships and sole trading companies are the forms of organisation for a business that are most frequently chosen by small or medium sized family companies. Reliance on the personal reputation and creditworthiness of the senior partner is an important factor in making this choice. Most partnerships enjoy a very good reputation in banking circles because of the personal liability of the senior partners. Partnerships trade under the names of their partners and all partners are personally responsible for the performance of contracts. The same is true for businessmen acting as sole traders. Therefore these organisational forms are very popular in Germany.

3.2.1 SOLE TRADERS

A one-man business can be run in two different ways: it is possible to register it as one-man limited company (GmbH) or as sole trader. The minimum capital that needs to be invested in a GmbH is DM 50,000 — an amount which can be prohibitive for smaller businesses. Therefore, the traditional form of commercial activity for small traders is the sole trading company. Anybody who carries out business under his or her own name can be a sole trader. A German peculiarity in this respect is the distinction made between 'minor' and 'major' traders. The commercial code (HGB) with its strict duties (regarding knowledge of commercial customs and efficiency of business organisation) only applies to the so-called major traders (*Vollkaufleute*). Minor traders cannot be registered and do not have such strict obligations. Article 1 of the Commercial Code contains a traditional list of who can be a major trader. The most important businesses listed are:

(1) Buying and selling goods.
(2) Trading with securities (not with land).
(3) Manufacturing of goods.

(4) Trade representatives.

Other types of trade can only be registered as major trades, if it is shown to the satisfaction of the registrar that the size of the business justifies registration (the criteria concern the necessity of bookkeeping, having several employees and the amount of bank credit needed). Building businesses and estate agents do not form part of the traditional group of major traders. When forming such a business it is therefore very important to check carefully on the duties regarding registration.

Formation procedure

There are no restrictions for the formation of a sole trading company. As a rule anyone may rent a shop and commence trading. Two notifications must be made:

(1) notification of the local trade authority; and
(2) notification of the local tax authority.

Some specialised trades are subject to permission by the local trade authority. These are amongst others:

(1) auctioneers;
(2) brokers;
(3) real estate developers; and
(4) casinos and gambling places.

Failure to register the sole trading company does not hinder its existence but may carry other disadvantages such as fines.

Company name

A sole trader must use his own name as his trading name. He may add a supplement indicating the nature of his business such as 'Hans Meier, Greengrocer' or 'Paul Schult, Leather Shoes'.

Representation

A sole trading company is represented by the proprietor. He can issue others with full or limited commercial power of attorney. However, a minor trader cannot issue full commercial power of attorney to another person.

Liability

Sole trading companies incur unrestricted personal liability for all debts and obligations which arise in the course of business. Therefore the creditors of a sole trader may seize both the company assets and his private assets.

Sale

The sale of a sole trading company is performed through the transfer of its assets to the purchaser. The 'goodwill' and the 'trading name' can only be sold together with the company. It is therefore possible for the purchaser to continue trading under the name of the original proprietor, eg, 'Hans Meier, Greengrocer, Proprietor, Paul Schult'.

Taxation Aspects

Profits or losses of sole traders are taxed together with the other income of the proprietor. The business profits are therefore subject to income tax. Trade tax and wealth tax (see Chapter 8) may also apply. Profits made from the sale of the business are subject to income tax. Individual tax privileges can be claimed where applicable.

3.2.2 GENERAL PARTNERSHIPS

German law knows two main types of commercial partnerships; limited partnerships (KG) and general partnerships (oHG). Both are based on the same basic principles. In either case several persons pursue a business purpose together. Each one of them has to make a contribution to the common goal, which can be either a financial contribution or a service (eg, accounting). It can also be sufficient that a wealthy person contributes to the partnership's creditworthiness by adding his name to the list of partners.

In a general partnership, all partners have equal rights and full liability whereas in a limited partnership some partners are fully liable whilst other partners can limit their liability to a fixed sum. Therefore one could say that a limited partnership (KG) is a somewhat more sophisticated variation of the normal general partnership (oHG). Accordingly, the principles governing a general partnership shall be examined first.

Formation

A partnership is created by contract to which all founding partners need to be a party. Although it is possible to conclude a partnership contract orally, most of them are drawn up by solicitors and contain complex articles of association. The partners often wish to deviate from the statutory law (HGB) that would otherwise govern their internal affairs (for example, HGB, Art 119 provides for one vote per partner — most partners prefer voting rights to be related to capital quotas).

A minimum capital is not required for the formation of a partnership, because all partners are fully liable to the company's creditors with all their personal assets. The following procedures have to be observed for the registration of the partnership:

(1) names of all partners;
(2) the name and seat of the partnership;
(3) the time when the partnership intends to commence trading; and
(4) notification of trade and tax authorities.

Company name

The company name must be made up of the names of the partners (eg, 'Meier and Muller'). It is sufficient to use one name only if a supplement indicates the existence of a partnership (eg, 'Meier & Co'). Further supplements describing the nature of the business may be added ('Meier & Partners Telephones').

Representation

As a rule all the partners have equal rights and equal standing in a general partnership. Therefore, each one of them may represent and conclude contracts on behalf of the company. Outsiders cannot normally be chosen as company representatives. Contractual provisions for joint representation may, however, be made. Such provisions need to be registered in the commercial register in order to be valid in third party dealings. Unregistered restrictions do not affect third parties which act in good faith.

Liability

The creditors of the general partnership can take legal action against both the partnership as such and against each individual partner. By virtue of HGB, Art 124 partnerships can be plaintiffs or defendants in court actions although they are strictly speaking not legal entities.

Other than in England, a judgment against the partnership cannot be enforced against a partner (and vice versa). Therefore it is highly advisable to sue both the company and its most creditworthy partners as joint defendants to secure a claim. The liability of a partner cannot be limited in any way. Bankruptcy of the company will, therefore, almost inevitably lead to all partners becoming insolvent as well.

Sales

As a rule of law a partner cannot sell his share in a partnership without prior permission by all other partners. However, it has now become common practice to allow the sale of partnerships in the articles of association.

Taxation

Profits and losses of the partnership are taxed as part of the private income of the partners after they have been distributed. This can be a disadvantage because of the way the company profits are calculated for the purposes of tax law. The cost of so-called partner contributions such as renting land to the company or rendering paid services to the company cannot be deducted from the profits of the partnership. Instead they will be fully taxed without any allowances for deducations.

Furthermore, the highest income tax (53 per cent) rate is slightly above the rate for corporation tax (50 per cent), which makes the partnership less attractive for a highly profitable business.

3.2.3 LIMITED PARTNERSHIPS

A general partnership will be transformed into a limited one, if some of the partners proceed to limit their liability in accordance with Art 170–175 of the Commercial Code. It is necessary, however, for one partner (the general partner) to remain fully liable.

The general partner does not have to be a natural person, he can also be a limited company (GmbH). In this case the limited partnership is called a GmbH & Co KG, and enjoys full limitation of liability. Its general partner is a legal entity that provides a limited capital only for the satisfaction of its creditors. The GmbH & Co KG is a German peculiarity, which enjoys great popularity because it combines the advantages of limitation of liability with the freedom to organise the company structure in a partnership contract.

Another increasingly popular type of limited partnership is the so-called mass partnership in which a large number of limited partners have a holding. Such companies often take the shape of investment companies or 'writing-off companies'. Writing-off companies produce yearly losses for their partners, which can be written off for tax purposes.

Formation procedure

To limit the liability of a partner, the partnership contract must name a fixed amount of money which the limited partner is willing to put into the company. This amount has to be registered and publicised and, subsequently, the liability of that particular partner will be limited to the registered amount. He does not need to produce the set sum immediately — it being sufficient for him to guarantee future payment. In this case, the creditors of the limited partnership can sue him directly for payment of the fixed sum.

Company name

The name of the general partner must be used in the company name. If the general partner is a legal entity (GmbH) this must also be shown. The names of limited partners must not be used in the company name.

Representation

To reflect their limited responsibility, the law restricts the rights of limited partners within the limited partnership. They cannot represent the KG unless they have obtained express authority from the general partner to do so, as the general partner is the only official representative of the partnership. His right to represent the company cannot be restricted. Limited partners are excluded from the management of the company unless the articles of association provide differently. However, all issues of outstanding importance for the company need to be decided by an assembly of all partners. Clauses attempting to abolish basic voting rights of limited partners, which are often made in mass partnerships, are void and therefore unenforceable. In the case of a GmbH & Co KG, the managing director of the GmbH represents the partnership. In most cases, he will also hold a share as a limited partner in the KG.

Liability

A limited partner can only lose the registered sum which he agreed to invest into the partnership. Once his contribution has been made in full, he has to fear no further liabilities unless he accepts payment from the partnership's assets in times where no profits have been made (repayment). In the latter case, he will be liable to the company's creditors up to the amount of repayment that he has received. General partners are fully liable, and their liability cannot be reduced or excluded.

Taxation

Taxation of profits in limited partnerships is identical with taxation in general partnerships (see above). Only a brief description of the structure of writing-off societies need therefore be given. Writing-off societies work with so-called 'negative accounts' for limited partners. A limited partner can accumulate losses (known as phantom losses), which exceed his capital holdings on his internal account without increasing his liability to company creditors. These losses are then set off against his income from other sources. To keep such activities under control, a new law now restricts the possibilities of setting off quite considerably. Basically, losses arising from shares in limited partnerships can only be set off against profits from the same source of income.

The benefits and drawbacks of partnerships are summarised in the following lists:

Benefits:

- Low formation and running costs.
- In principle no publicity and auditing obligations.
- No co-determination of employees.
- No double tax burden for wealth and trade tax.
- Easy to supply capital.
- Compensation of losses between company and partners possible.
- Foreign shareholders have the full benefits of setting off tax.

Drawbacks:

- No restriction of liability.
- No separation of investment and management function possible.
- Salary payments to partners are not tax deductible.

- Complicated mechanism for distribution of profits.
- Difficult to transfer holdings.
- Church tax payable.
- No international affiliation relief.

3.2.4 SILENT PARTNERSHIPS

The silent partnership is closely related to a loans or credit contract. Instead of receiving interest on the sum lent, the silent partner receives a share in the profits of another person's business in exchange for his investment. Like a money lender, he does not run the risk of losing more than the invested sum, because it is not necessary for him to participate in the losses of the business.

The silent partner is not known to the outside world as a business partner and all third party dealings are handled exclusively by the owner of the business. Secrecy and anonymity are viewed as major advantages of a silent partnership. Such partnerships can be used to provide a member of the family with a source of income without having to involve that person in the management of the business.

Formation

Silent partnerships are created by contract, which should be made in writing. The parties are free to allocate the size of the silent holding and the rights of the silent partner, according to their liking, in the articles of association. Thus, the silent partner can be made the internal manager of the company by requiring his approval for all external transactions (a typical silent partnership). As the partnership is silent or secret, no registration is required and the company is run under the name of the proprietor without any mention of the name of the silent partner.

Liability

As the silent partnership is not revealed to the outside world, third parties can only contract with and sue the proprietor. The silent investment is treated as part of the proprietor's assets for these purposes. As there is no privity of contract between the silent partner and third parties, the silent partner cannot be held personally liable for company debts.

Taxation aspects

For the purposes of taxation, a silent partner can be treated like a full partner, if it is shown that he is the true managing partner. In this case, his income is treated as commercial income and not as capital investment income. As a result, tax is chargeable if 'silent reserves' (hidden gains which do not appear in the balance sheet) are realised. The creation of typical silent partnerships can also serve as a useful tool to avoid inheritance tax, which can be very high in Germany (up to 70 per cent). Children can accrue considerable assets over the years which will not be subject to inheritance tax, if they are made silent partners at an early age.

3.3 LIMITED COMPANIES AND PUBLIC LIMITED COMPANIES

Company forms, which are based on the idea of co-operation between a small number of individual persons with equal standing, have been explained above.

The second form of business organisation which almost every legal system provides is the legal person or legal entity. It provides anonymity for the individual shareholder and does not involve them personally in the company management. Two types of legal entities are particularly widespread in Germany: the limited company (GmbH) and the public limited company (AG). Other more specialised forms of organisation exist for insurances (VVaG) and for cooperatives (eG).

Today the GmbH (limited company) is the most popular organisational form for small to medium sized businesses in Germany. AGs (public limited companies) are designed to meet the needs of large businesses which wish to have their stocks quoted on the market.

3.3.1 GMBH (LIMITED COMPANY)

The GmbH is often called the joint stock company of the little man, because it fulfils many functions of a public limited company within a simplified legal structure. The German law governing a GmbH is considerably more flexible than the law dealing with public limited companies. A GmbH can be founded and owned by a single person and the minimum capital needed to effect registration is only DM 50,000, up to 50 per cent of which may be inserted by non-cash contributions. Most of the several hundred thousands GmbHs that exist in Germany start business with no more than the minimum capital.

Formation procedure

To achieve limitation of their liability, the founders of a GmbH have to observe a formal foundation procedure. The following list illustrates the different stages in the formation of a GmbH.

(1) Contract sealed by a notary containing:
  (a) the company name;
  (b) the object of the company;
  (c) the amount of capital stock; and
  (d) the amount which is to be paid by each shareholder.

(2) Insertion of assets:
  (a) founders must insert one quarter of the promised capital but not less than DM 25,000 at once;
  (b) single founders have to provide security for missing assets.

(3) Application for registration (usually arranged by the notary) containing:
  (a) the foundation contract;
  (b) a list of shareholders;
  (c) a report on cash assets;
  (d) a valuation report on non-cash assets; and
  (e) a declaration that the minimum capital has been paid in.

(4) Registration. The registrar enters the new limited company into the registry.

(5) The GmbH commences its legal existence.

The procedure described above can take considerable time (incomplete applications might have to be amended) during which a quasi-company with some assets, which does not yet have the status of a legal entity exists. This quasi-GmbH can already commence business, but there will be no limitation of liability until full registration has been effected. Therefore, all founders and other persons involved will be strictly liable for all debts incurred before registration.

Company name

The naming of a GmbH leaves room for imagination, because both the founders' names and the object of the company can be used, either combined or separately, to create an attractive trading name (eg, 'Purple Sunshine Travel GmbH'). The letters 'mbH' must always be added after the name, because they indicate the limitation of liability.

Organisation

The GmbH is represented by one or more managing directors who are appointed by the shareholders, but need not themselves be shareholders. It is not possible to limit the power of attorney of the managing director of a GmbH. Internal restrictions may be imposed, but they cannot be enforced against third parties.

Liabilities

As soon as a GmbH has been registered, the liability is restricted to the company's assets. Personal liability of managing directors and shareholders is only possible if irregularities have occurred. This is the case if the GmbH has not been provided with enough capital (under-capitalisation), and the shareholders try to insert capital as loans instead. Such loans can be seized by the company's creditors. The repayment of capital to the shareholders will also lead to liabilities. Extreme cases of fraudulent abuse of the legal form of a GmbH have led to further examples of direct personal liability.

Sale

Shares in a GmbH are freely transferable. A notarial document is required to complete the assignment.

Taxation and other costs

Several different taxes and costs become due during the foundation of a GmbH.

(1) Capital transfer tax (1 per cent of the shares).
(2) Land transfer duty in case of land assets (2 per cent of the unit value).
(3) Turnover tax is *not* payable.
(4) Accountancy costs for founders' reports and valuation of non-cash assets.
(5) Notary costs (minimum of DM 500).
(6) Registration fee (negligible).

The sale or assignment of shares involves the following tax and costs:

(1) Income tax on profits (full tax for commercial owners and

speculation tax only for private owners).
(2) Land transfer tax if land is involved.
(3) Notary costs.

The profits of the GmbH itself are subject to corporation tax at the standard rate of 50 per cent. Other than in the case of partnerships, salaries paid to managing directors will reduce the profit. Trade tax and wealth tax are also payable whenever dividends are paid out to the shareholders, the fact that a corporation tax of 50 per cent has already been paid on the profits is taken into account to avoid double taxation. Persons who pay less than 50 per cent income tax will therefore receive reimbursement.

3.3.2 THE AG (PUBLIC LIMITED COMPANY)

The AG is the only company which has a capital that is divided into shares, which can be quoted on the market. The AG is therefore comparable to the British public limited company in many respects. Some companies such as mortgage banks and capital investment companies must be organised in the form of an AG, while insurances have an option between an AG and a VVaG. Most banks (Deutsche Bank AG, Dresdner Bank AG) are organised as AGs.

At the end of 1987 there were some 2,500 public limited companies registered in Germany, while only 471 of them had their shares quoted on the stock exchange. Others are family companies with all shares held by the members of a single family. The formation of a one-man AG is also possible but extremely rare.

Formation procedure

The creation of an AG is governed by numerous strict formation rules that are designed to protect the future shareholders and creditors of the company. As with the formation of a GmbH, different stages can be distinguished:

(1) Drawing up of a foundation contract:
   (a) A minimum of five founders are required who can be either Germans or foreigners.
   (b) Notarial documentation is needed.
   (c) Articles of association must contain; shares and capital stock (minimum DM 100,000), the face value and

number of the shares (minimum 2,000 × DM 50), the issue price of the shares (minimum face value), and the shares to be held by each of the founders.

(d) A company description must include; the name and location of the company, the object of the company, and the names of members of the board of directors.

Other details may be necessary depending on the type of shares issued.

(2) Purchasing of the shares. After the conclusion of the foundation contract the founders must purchase all the shares (a stayed formation is not possible).

(3) Appointment of the first members of:
   (a) The supervisory board (a board which controls the activities of the board of directors).
   (b) The auditors.
   (c) The board of directors.

(4) Written formation report:
   (a) A detailed report on (1) to (3) must be given. Non-cash investments must be detailed and justified.
   (b) Purchase of shares on behalf of board members must be explained.
   (c) A copy of the report must be submitted to the local Chambers of Commerce which will issue a certificate.

(5) Registration. The AG is to be registered by all founders and all board members. The application for registration must include:
   (a) Articles of association.
   (b) Any special privileges which have been granted.
   (c) A report on non-cash investments.
   (d) Documentation on the appointment of all board members.
   (e) A formation report.
   (f) A copy of the certificate issued by the local Chambers of Commerce.
   (g) If a licence is needed, a copy of the licensing certificate.
   (h) Evidence to show that the sum paid in for the shares is at the free disposal of the board of directors (bank confirmation).

(6) The AG comes into existence. If the registrar is satisfied that all the above requirements have been met, he will enter the

AG into the commercial register. As a result the AG achieves full legal existence.

(7) Shares may now be transferred and interim certificates issued.

Company name

The name of the AG should reflect the nature of the company's business. Personal names can only be used under exceptional circumstances. Foreign names are permitted if they are comprehensible or officially recognised in the relevant branch of industry (management company, or holding company).

Internal structure of the AG

The German AG has a quasi democratic structure which is characterised by a sophisticated system of checks and balances. Three major representative organs can be distinguished:

(1) the board of directors;
(2) the supervisory board; and
(3) the general meeting of all shareholders.

The board of directors. The board of directors manages and represents the AG. It is here that most major commercial decisions are made. The board is made up of one or more natural persons, who are appointed by the supervisory board. Legal entities like a GmbH cannot be members of the board of directors. Several directors manage the company jointly. In this case it is common to appoint one person as Head Director or Managing Director of the Board (*Vorstandsvorsitzender*).

Although the activities of the directors are submitted to the internal control of the supervisory board, their power to represent the AG externally towards third parties cannot be restricted. A director may, however, be liable to pay compensation to the company, if he transgressed his internal duties or limitations.

The supervisory board. The supervisory board supervises the activities of the board of directors and protects the interests of the shareholders. As a rule the members of the supervisory board are elected for a period of four years by the shareholders in their annual general meeting. However, large AGs with more than 500 employees are subject to laws regulating co-determination rights of employees. In this case, the employees have the right to be represented on the supervisory board (see Chapter 7):

The general meeting. Each year a general meeting of the shareholders has to be called by the board of directors. A demand for an extraordinary meeting can be made by shareholders holding 5 per cent of the stock.

A number of very important decisions concerning the structure and the development of the company cannot be made without the approval of the general meeting. These decisions include:

(1) Appointment of members to the supervisory board;
(2) Decisions about the use of the annual profits;
(3) Amendments to the articles of association;
(4) Reduction of the capital stock;
(5) Issuing of new shares;
(6) Changing the object of the company.

Decisions are made by votes. Voting rights depend on the face value of the shares. Some shares do not provide the right to vote (so-called preferential shares).

If most of the shares are held by small shareholders, banks will often exercise their voting rights for them. The shareholder can instruct his bank on how he wishes to vote, but generally small shareholders follow the voting proposals made by their banks. Therefore most large German banks (especially the Deutsche Bank AG) have powerful voting capacities in the general meetings of many public limited companies.

Each individual shareholder has the right to attend the general meeting and to receive information on the company policies from the board of directors. Such information may only be withheld in special cases. Furthermore, if irregularities occur a shareholder can apply to the court for annulment of a decision made by the general meeting.

Liability

An AG is a legal person and therefore liable to all its creditors as such. Members of the board of directors and members of the supervisory board can incur personal liability if they violate their obligations. In accordance with Art 93 of the law governing public limited companies, all board members have to apply the care of a conscientious business man in managing the company. Any breach of this duty resulting in losses for the company will mean that they have to reimburse the AG. Strict rules apply for insolvency. Announcement of pending insolvency must be made as soon as it becomes clear that the company cannot be rescued. Any further delay will result in personal liability of the responsible board members.

Sale of shares

Shares in public limited companies are freely transferable. As most shares are kept in bank deposits, the transfer is usually executed by changing the depository records. Shares which are quoted on the stock market will usually be sold through registered brokers.

Taxation

The following taxes and costs have to be expected when founding the company:

Taxes:

(1) Incorporation tax of 1 per cent of the share capital.
(2) Land transfer duty in case of real estate assets.
(3) Currently *no* stock transfer tax applies.

Costs:

(1) Notary cost (for an AG worth DM 6 million the cost would be DM 30,000).
(2) Formation report costs (DM 5,000).
(3) Registration costs (very low).

The following taxes apply to profits and turnover.

(1) As a rule corporation tax of 50 per cent is payable on all profits made by the AG.
(2) Profits which are distributed to the shareholders (dividend) are taxable at a rate of 36 per cent. The individual shareholder is entitled to a refund if his personal income tax rate is lower than 36 per cent. He must pay the difference if his personal tax is above that amount.
(3) Wealth tax at a rate of 0.6 per cent is payable on the company's assets.
(4) Turnover tax applies.

3.3.3 VVaG and eG, Reederei

Insurance companies are usually organised as VVaG (mutual insurance company) whereas cooperatives can use the eG as their organisational structure. Both are legal entitles which are regulated by special laws. The Reederei is a type of partnership which can be used by joint owners of one or several vessels. It is regulated in the commercial code.

3.4 THE EEIG

Since 1 July 1989, a new European form of company, the so-called European Economic Industry Grouping (EEIG) exists in all EEC member countries. Germany has implemented the EEC Directive No 2137–85 by means of an EEIG Law which regulates the formation and management of an EEIG in accordance with the Directive. EEIGs are intended to provide a suitable organisational form for joint ventures between small and medium-sized companies from different EEC member states.

Formation

Two or more persons who pursue a trade in different EEC member states can form an EEIG. National EEIGs can therefore not be formed. The founding contract must contain:

(1) The name and location of the EEIG.
(2) The object and duration of the EEIG.
(3) The members names.

The seat of the EEIG must be in a member state. The EEIG has to be registered in the commercial register, if its seat is going to be in Germany. After registration, the EEIG can conclude contracts in its own name.

Representation and structure

In Germany, the EEIG is treated in a similar way as a general partnership. It can, therefore, be the bearer of rights although it is not a legal entity. The EEIG acts through its managing directors, who can represent the company either jointly or severally. The form of representation chosen has to be published in the *Federal Gazette*.

Liability

No minimum capital is required to form an EEIG. Therefore, it may lack assets of its own. Consequently all members of an EEIG are fully liable to the company's creditors.

Taxation

The EEIG itself is not liable to pay tax on profits. Article 40 of the EEC Directive provides; 'The results of the activities of the Association are only taxable from its members'.

Therefore, each member is taxed according to his or her national tax law. However, German turnover tax may be applicable. The application of German trade tax is still a matter of dispute.

3.5 Disclosure provisions

The German commercial code now contains a large new section which aims to implement the recent EEC directives on disclosure. As a result all large AGs and some of the very large partnerships are now obliged to publish their accounts. The disclosure obligations for smaller partnerships and sole traders have also been increased. The following details have to be published for large partnerships:

(1) proceeds from turnover;
(2) proceeds from holdings;
(3) wages, pension, maintenance costs;
(4) valuation methods; and
(5) the number of employees

The profit and loss calculation does not have to be published, neither does the overall result and the way the profits are used. An AG has to publish the following facts regardless of its size:

(1) balance sheet;
(2) list of all shareholders;
(3) profit and loss calculation;
(4) situation report;
(5) auditing note;
(6) report of the supervisory board;
(7) annual profits; and
(8) proposals and decisions on how to use those profits.

The exact extent of these obligations depends on the size of the AG. For medium-sized (those with a balance sheet total of DM 3.9 million to DM 15.5 million and between 50 and 250 employees) and large AGs (with a balance sheet total in excess of DM 15.5 million and over 250 employees) there is a deadline for disclosure of nine months, whereas for small AGs (with a balance sheet total below DM 3.9 million and fewer than 50 employees) the deadline for disclosure is 12 months and the requirement for the disclosure of the profit and loss calculation is relaxed.

Because of the extent of these obligations, some businessmen may find it advisable to choose a GmbH & Co KG, rather than an AG to organise a company. In the case of a GmbH & Co KG the laws governing limited partnerships apply. Only the figures concerning the GmbH which are usually of little significance for the whole of the business must be published in this event.

4
MERGERS AND ACQUISITIONS

4.1 INTRODUCTION

There is no separate legal code governing the purchase of companies in Germany. Therefore, the ways and means of acquiring companies are as diverse as the types of companies which can be purchased.

As a result, mergers and acquisitions under German law can be highly complicated legal procedures. A variety of different statutory laws will have to be observed, including:

- Law of Property.
- Law of Contract.
- Commercial Law.
- Company Law.
- Cartel Law.
- Labour Law.

As far as acquisitions are concerned, the laws mentioned are often incomplete or impracticable, and so it is absolutely essential that comprehensive contractual agreements are drawn up to clarify the position of the parties and avoid legal disputes.

In 1990, more than 2,700 purchase transactions were recorded in Germany, with prices fluctuating between five to eight times the pre-tax profit.

4.2 THE OBJECT OF A COMPANY PURCHASE

As described in Chapter 3, there is no such thing as a 'company' which can be the object of a 'company purchase' under German law. In the legal sense, the word 'company' does not exist. Instead, a company is perceived by the law as a collection of movable and immovable objects, rights and obligations, goodwill and resources. Nevertheless, it is recognised by German courts that a company as a whole is the commercial object of the sales contract. Two ways of purchasing a company can be distinguished.

The sale is either made by transferring the individual company assets to the purchaser (asset deal or singular succession) or by purchasing shares in a company (purchase of a holding). The latter possibility is only available where the company structure allows for the formation of shares. Accordingly, sole trading companies can only be purchased by an asset deal.

The company may be transferred in full or only partly. Thus, it is possible to purchase a local branch or a single manufacturing unit of a larger business only. It is also possible to purchase minority and majority shares.

4.3 THE PURCHASE OF ASSETS

This type of company purchase involves the transfer of all individual assets to the purchaser one by one. This may result in considerable practical difficulties, which can only be mastered through the use of sophisticated contractual clauses.

Negative limitation

It is often best to clarify first of all which items the purchaser does not wish to receive:

Private assets. In the case of sole trading companies there is often no delineation between private and company assets (often the wife of the proprietor has full use of the 'company car' or privately owned land is used for business purposes).

The civil ownership situation is not always reflected correctly in the company's balance sheets. It is therefore useful to list the items which the buyer does not wish to receive.

Unwanted assets. Other commercial assets which are not required should also be listed separately, (eg, unsaleable old stocks, outdated machinery).

Positive description

The next step is a clear description of all physical goods which are to be transferred, so that they can be identified individually by the purchaser. The quantity and quality of the items involved needs to be described, with only minor simplifications being possible (eg, 'all boxes of wine stored in room 10'). Otherwise the lawyer has the tedious task of preparing extensive lists of assets. Security rights of banks and suppliers of goods must also be observed.

Transfer of liabilities and contractual obligations

The purchaser of a company usually takes over the legal obligations of the seller together with his company rights and assets. Whilst the purchaser is free to accept joint liability for such obligations together with the seller, he will need the consent of all creditors involved in order to replace the vendor. It should therefore be clarified in advance whether such consent can be obtained (eg, the consent of the landlord in the case of a lease of company premises).

Industrial property rights

The transfer of intellectual property rights is subject to some restrictions:

(1) Trademarks can only be transferred with the company to which they belong and the transfer must be registered in the trademark register.
(2) Copyrights cannot be transferred to another person, although licences can be issued.
(3) Expertise which is not protected by law can be described and protected by contract and transferred accordingly. It is usually wise to include a provision in the contract which prevents the vendor from using such expertise himself in the future.

Employees

According to Art 613 (*a*) of the Civil Code, the company purchaser automatically becomes party to all existing employment contracts by virtue of the law. The termination of such contracts because of a company purchase is statutorily prohibited (see Chapter 7).

The company as a whole

There is more to the purchase and transfer of the company than the legal transfer of individual assets. Therefore, an additional clause which provides for the transfer of the entire company will also be needed. This clause should refer to such matters as goodwill, introduction to existing business contacts, explanation of marketing schemes, and other non-material assets.

4.4 THE PURCHASE OF A HOLDING

The purchase of a holding greatly simplifies the procedure of a company purchase. Shares in a GmbH or AG are freely transferable and the basic rule is that they can be assigned in the same manner as any other rights.

4.4.1 HOLDINGS AND LEGAL ENTITIES

When purchasing a holding in a GmbH (limited company) or AG (public limited company) certain formalities have to be observed. Thus, the sale of GmbH shares requires notarial documentation. The same requirement applies to the sale of shares in a limited partnership which has a GmbH as its general partner (GmbH & Co KG).

Before shares in a GmbH are transferred, an interim balance sheet is drawn up to determine the level of profits on the date of transfer. This serves to determine the distribution of the current profits between the vendor and the purchaser.

4.4.2 HOLDINGS AND PARTNERSHIPS

The purchase of a holding in a partnership is slightly more complicated because, strictly speaking, partners are joint proprietors rather than shareholders in the company. (See Section **3.5**.) Obligations of a non-financial nature are attached to a holding in a partnership. It is therefore recommended that a contractual list of all rights and obligations is drawn up with corresponding guarantees of correctness (see also Section **4.7**).

The contract should also provide for the settlement of any losses on the vendor's company account. Losses can be settled by reducing the purchase price. Profits can be split or paid out to the vendor.

4.5 ADDITIONAL CONSIDERATIONS FOR A COMPANY PURCHASE

Fiscal considerations and questions of competition law will often have a strong influence on the exact structure of a company purchase contract.

4.5.1 SUPERVISION OF MERGERS

Notification might have to be given to the Cartels' Authority if a company purchase leads to a merger which fulfils the requirements for fusion control under the GWB (see Section 2.2).

If there are reasons to believe that the Cartels' Authority will raise objections against the purchase, it is advisable to consult them at an early stage to establish the conditions which will have to be fulfilled to make the merger acceptable.

4.5.2 FISCAL CONSIDERATIONS

From the fiscal point of view, there is a basic difference between the purchase of a partnership and the purchase of shares in a legal entity. When purchasing a holding in a limited company, the balance sheets and book values which relate to the firm's assets remain unaffected by the transaction. In contrast to that, the agreed purchase price for a partnership share causes a change in the company's accounting values.

These effects can be used to gain tax advantages for the vendor or purchaser. Often the interest of one party is contrary to the interests of the other party in this respect. It is, therefore, very important to get sound advice from an accountant on the tax implications of the transaction prior to choosing a particular modality of a purchase contract.

4.5.3 LICENCES

When purchasing a company which requires a public licence for its commercial activities (examples are broking companies, casinos, hospitals) the purchaser needs to ensure that he fulfils the conditions for the continuance of the public licence. In case of doubt, it may be wise to insert a clause into the contract which protects the purchaser's position.

4.5.4 LETTER OF INTENT

German law does not recognise the 'letter of intent' as anything but a declaration on the contents of pre-contractual negotiations. Protection for the parties against the sudden breaking off of negotiations is provided by the concept of *culpa in contrahendo* which gives the disappointed party an action for damages against the other party. It has to be shown that the negotiations were broken off without reasonable cause — a letter of intent can be strong evidence to support such an allegation. It is, therefore, recommended not to conclude letters of intent and instead, a preliminary contract should be created which should contain regulations that provide for the failure of the negotiations. It should also contain obligations concerning secrecy and preliminary examination rights of the purchaser.

4.6 LIABILITY

The extent to which the purchaser of a company is liable for debts which were incurred before the purchase date, depends on a number of different factors. Whilst few liabilities run with the purchase of shares in legal entities, the new owner of a sole trading company or a partnership can experience some unpleasant surprises.

4.6.1 LIABILITY FOR CONTINUATION OF COMPANY NAME

If the purchaser in an asset deal continues the business under the same company name, he may be liable for all debts of the former proprietor (HGB, Art 25). This rule aims to protect the company's creditors because the continuation of the name might lead them to believe that they are still dealing with the same proprietor. Slight amendments to the name do not affect this statutory liability. The purchaser has two choices to avoid his liability. He can either effect immediate registration and publication of a limitation on his liability, a step which needs the consent of the vendor, or he can choose to abandon the company name. The latter solution is often not commercially viable because the name is closely connected with the goodwill of the company.

If neither solution suits the purposes of the purchaser, he should employ an independent accountant to inspect the company's accounts before completion of the takeover, in order to be able to predict possible liabilities under Art 25.

4.6.2 LIABILITY ACCORDING TO ART 419 OF THE CIVIL CODE

If a company constitutes almost all the assets of the vendor (80–90 per cent), the purchaser may be held liable for both the vendor's private and his business debts (Art 419 of the Civil Code). This liability cannot be restricted. Thus, the regulation of Art 419 represents a major risk for the purchaser and it applies to all types of asset deals, provided that the vendor has no private property of considerable value left after completion of the transaction. Again, caution must therefore be taken to ensure that the vendor retains other properties. It is often a good strategy to postpone the payment of parts of the purchase price for an interim period to see if any unknown creditors attempt to bring claims under Art 419.

4.6.3 PURCHASER'S LIABILITY FOR UNPAID TAXES

The purchaser of a company may be held liable for the payment of taxes which run with the company, such as trade tax, value added tax and excise duty, because these tax obligations are founded on the operation of the company.

4.6.4 PARTNERSHIP SHARES

General partner

If the position of a general partner is transferred, the purchaser may be held fully liable for all existing and future company debts without any restrictions. This liability is compulsory and cannot be limited. As a result, general partnerships are not normally purchased.

Limited partnerships

The purchase of a limited partnership is more commonly encountered as it is possible to clarify the question of liability by simply observing a number of steps.

First of all, the purchaser needs to ensure that the limited share has been paid in in full. Next, he has to register his succession to the previous partner in the Commercial Register.

As a consequence, he will now be given credit for the contributions of the former partner and his liability will be limited to the same amount.

If he fails to obtain immediate registration, he may be held fully liable for all debts that are incurred by the partnership up to the day of his registration.

If the share of the previous partner has not been paid in in full, the purchaser may be held liable for the missing amount. Since it is very difficult in practice to establish whether a company account became negative because of losses incurred during the course of business or because of failure to pay in the full contribution, the purchaser should secure his position by obtaining a contractual guarantee on this point.

4.6.5 GmbH SHARES AND STOCKS

Whilst stocks are sold on the stock exchange in Frankfurt, the sale of GmbH shares is usually executed individually.

The purchaser of GmbH shares can be held liable for the following payments:

(1) Outstanding contributions towards the capital stock.
(2) In case of over-valuation of non-cash assets by the founders, for payment of the difference in value.
(3) Additional cash injections, if the articles of association provide for them.
(4) Repayment of illegal dividends that have been distributed though no profits were made.

4.7 GUARANTEES

4.7.1 STATUTORY LAW

Germany has no law governing guarantees for company purchases. To fill this gap, the Federal Court of Justice has applied statutory regulations dealing with the purchase of goods (Art 459–480 of the Civil Code) for the purchase of both company holdings and company assets. According to these rules, the vendor of an object is deemed to have guaranteed that the object is free from any faults and defects. A company is generally viewed as defective if false representations about its earning capacity have been made. There is a large number of precedents on this subject dealing mainly with incorrect balance sheets and over-valuation of assets. Difficulties occur when a holding is purchased, because it cannot be said that the company with all its assets was the object of the purchase contract, unless the holding was a clear majority holding in the company. For smaller holdings of 50 per cent and less, this question has not yet been finally clarified by the German courts.

4.7.2 CONTRACTUAL GUARANTEES

The difficulties outlined above have led to the creation of comprehensive contractual guarantees. These guarantees usually cover:

(1) Express guarantees of all important properties of the company such as:
  - (a) statements concerning the potential earning power of the company;
  - (b) statements concerning the correctness of the balance sheet;
  - (c) statements concerning the correctness of the valuation of the company assets;
  - (d) comprehensive checklists of all circumstances which the purchaser considers important; and a
  - (e) list of negative statements.

(2) Guarantees for client connections and other structures can also be required.

A well-worded guarantee will serve to ensure the strict liability of the vendor for all guaranteed items. However, it must be taken into account that some major financial factors are difficult to describe in a guarantee. For example, the success of pending deals, the result of delivery orders which have been issued or received, the continuation of credit agreements and other pending deals cannot be guaranteed.

The contract should also fix the legal consequences of non-observance of any of the guarantees. Often a choice between a right of reduction of the purchase price and a right to repudiate the contract is provided for.

5
AGENCY, FRANCHISING AND RELATED DISTRIBUTION CONTRACTS

5.1 INTRODUCTION

German law offers a wide variety of legal structures for the distribution of goods and services. The most important of these structures will be examined in the following chapter. The list below illustrates the most commonly encountered distribution structures:

(1) Agency systems: which includes branches, networks of commercial representatives, and the use of agents for commission or mercantile brokers.

(2) Franchising: this includes goods franchising, services franchising and know-how franchising.

(3) Other systems which are frequently encountered are home traders and branches of foreign companies.

5.2 AGENCY

German law knows two different concepts of agency: disclosed and undisclosed agency. In both cases an agent acts on behalf of a principal. In the case of disclosed or proper agency, the agent reveals that he is acting on behalf of someone else, in which case the principal will usually have to be named. Disclosed agency, or agency for commission, is characterised by the fact that the principal remains unknown. German law allows no privity of contract between an unknown principal and a third party. Therefore, disclosed agency involves two contracts, a contract between the agent and the third party and another contract between the agent and the principal which transfers the right obtained from the third party to the principal.

Another distribution system which is based on the concept

of agency is the branch system. It uses the method of disclosed agency.

5.2.1 BRANCHES

A branch of a company is a part of that company which has a certain amount of organisational independence, although a branch does not constitute a separate legal entity. The branch is managed by an employee of the company, who has authority to act on behalf of the company as principal with regard to all matters concerning the branch. Although branches do not have their own legal identity they are given a number of independent rights. They can be sued and registered at their seat. They can also be sold independently. These provisions are designed to reflect the fact that individual customers often mistake local branches of major companies for independent units. The necessary contracts which are needed to set up a branch are concluded by the head company through the branch manager as their agent. Banks and supermarkets are traditionally organised in branches in Germany.

5.2.2 COMMERCIAL REPRESENTATIVES

A commercial representative is an independent trader who acts as agent for other companies. He concludes contracts and arranges business contracts for the other company as his principal. The commercial representative runs his own business and is therefore not an employee of the principal he acts for. As a result he is self-employed and self-insured. He has to maintain his own offices and pay his own expenses. This makes the distribution of a product through trade representative an attractive alternative to the branch system. The position of a trade representative is protected by statutory regulations contained in the Commercial Code. Most of the protective rights and obligations cannot be altered in the contract.

The relationship of the commercial representative to the company

An agency contract with a commercial representative can be concluded either orally or in writing. Usually larger companies will provide standard forms for such contracts. When setting up a new system of commercial representatives, it is advisable to have such contracts drawn up by solicitors. The advice of a solicitor is very important for both parties because the statutory law governing their relationship consists of a confusing combination of rules of law which can or cannot be altered contractually.

Rights and duties of the trade representative

The framework for an agency contract as it is set out by the law consists of the following duties and obligations:

Loyalty. Since a trade representative acts on behalf of someone else, it is his first and most important duty to look after the interests of the principal when concluding a transaction for him (known as the duty of loyalty).

He must, therefore, not contract with unsuitable customers. He has to observe his duty of secrecy and he must not pass documentation entrusted to him to any third parties.

Information. A representative has to pass information on all transactions concluded by him to the principal, on whose behalf they have been made.

Commission. The representative receives a special commission for every business transaction which has been successfully completed. Some representatives will also guarantee the correct performance of the contract. In this case an additional *del credere commission* has to be paid. These rights cannot be excluded contractually. Some representatives also receive a basic minimum salary, which is paid out to them regardless of the amount of commission due.

Compensation claim. On termination of the contract the representative has a right to payment of compensation. This payment is designed to compensate for the financial value of the business contacts that he has built up for the principal. The amount due is usually calculated on the basis of his annual commission earnings. Consideration is also given to the duration of the contract. The total amount is at the discretion of the court.

Duties of the company

Support. The company has to support the agent by providing him with the necessary documentation that he requires for his work.

Loyalty. Although the company can refuse to perform contracts concluded by a trade representative, such refusal must be based on good reasons. Otherwise commission will be payable even if the contract is not carried out.

Termination

The contract can be terminated at the end of a quarter, with a notice period of six weeks according to statutory law. This period may be contractually abbreviated to one month. Contracts of more than three years' duration have a statutory notice period of three months, which can also be abbreviated. Extraordinary termination without notice is possible if either party is guilty of grave misconduct, such as fraud or theft or other serious offenses.

For the period after termination, a ban on competitive activities will usually have been inserted in the initial contract. In this event, a reasonable compensation payment has to be made to the trade representative.

The relationship of the trade representative to third parties

The representative is an agent for the company as principal and, therefore, there is no privity of contract between him and third parties who he deals with on behalf of the company. All contracts are concluded directly between such parties and the principal.

However, the representative can be personally liable to such parties under the doctrine of *culpa in contrahendo*, if he offers a personal guarantee for the correct performance of the contract or the quality of the goods. In the case of a fraud committed by the representative, both the company and the representative can be liable to the third party.

EEC law and international law

The implementation of EEC Directive 382–17 has led to the creation of a new species of trade representatives, the so-called general representative. He is an entrepreneur in his own right within a multi-stage distribution organisation with 'subrepresentatives' acting for him. General representatives are often used by foreign companies wishing to enter the German market.

German law applies to trade representative contracts, if the representative is based in Germany. Otherwise foreign law will be applicable. Representatives that act outside the territory of the EEC are not protected by German law.

Dispute settlement

Disputes between representatives and the company they act for have to be settled before the labour courts if the representative acts for one company only, and has a monthly income of DM 2,000 only (so-called small trade representatives).

If the trade representative earns more than DM 2,000 per month, or acts for several different principals, the Chambers of Commerce have jurisdiction.

5.2.3 COMMISSION AGENTS

Unlike a trade representative, a commission agent buys or sells goods in his own name, but on behalf of another person whose identity is not disclosed. A classical commission contract will usually involve a sale of an individual object through a commissioner (such as the sale of old family jewellery through an antique shop). However, commission contracts can also be used as the framework for a constant business relationship. The commission system has the advantage of secrecy, because the name of the principal does not have to be disclosed to the customer. There is no direct contact and no privity of contract between the principal and the customer. As a result the commission agent will initially acquire ownership of all goods purchased on behalf of his principal. Sophisticated legal clauses have been drawn up to eliminate the potential risks arising from this situation. In spite of these attempts, commission agency remains fairly unpopular as a system for long-term distribution.

The commission agent has the usual duties regarding secrecy and loyalty. He must follow the instructions of his principal and he is liable for damages if he deviates from them.

The principal has to pay the agreed commission to the agent and reimburse him for his expenses.

5.2.4 BROKERS

Brokers act as independent intermediaries for commercial contracts. They bring the potential vendor and purchaser together and prepare the contract for them. In the event that the contract is successfully concluded, they earn a commission, which will often be a percentage of the total amount involved.

Duties of a commercial broker

The duties of a commercial broker are regulated in Arts 94–97 of the Commercial Code. These rules subject the broker to extensive obligations regarding secrecy and loyalty to the interests of his client. In particular, a broker must not act on behalf of both the vendor and the purchaser, unless he has been given express permission to do so. Upon conclusion of the contract the broker must provide both parties with a 'broker's note', which has to contain a statement on the contents of the transaction which has been completed, as well as the quantity and quality of the goods sold and the purchase price.

Rights of a commercial broker

The commercial broker has a right to claim payment of the agreed remuneration as soon as the intended contract has been concluded. If the contractual negotiations fail, the broker loses his pay, unless he has protected his position by a special payment agreement. If the client causes the broker unnecessary expense, or demands unusual services, a separate remuneration can be due.

5.3 Franchise contracts

The franchise contract has only recently entered German law, after its development and initial success in Anglo-American countries led to the formation of franchise systems all over the world. Consequently, there is no German word for 'franchising' and the traditional categories of law do not apply. Franchise concepts open up particularly good possibilities for gaining access to foreign markets. They have therefore experienced a considerable boom in Germany over the last few years. Franchising is used by foreign companies (Body Shop, MacDonalds, Tie Rack) to enter the German market by means of allocating so-called master franchise licences for the entire country to legally independent subsidiaries.

Generally speaking, a franchise contract is concluded between two independent companies and provides for one company (the franchisor) to grant the other company (the franchisee) the right to operate a particular sales and marketing concept in exchange for monetary consideration. By such a contract, the franchisee must use the company name, trade name, sales and advertising methods and expertise of the franchisor, in order to be allowed to sell its goods.

The franchisee has to display the franchise products in the same manner as the other franchisees. He has to trade under the same trading name and use the decoration and presentation methods prescribed by the franchisor. Franchise contracts can be concluded for the sale of goods, for the promotion of services and for the exploitation of knowhow. Therefore, the legal framework for franchise contracts can vary considerably.

5.3.1 THE APPLICABLE LAW

German law provides no statute governing the contractual relationship between the franchisee and the franchisor. Therefore, the parties are free to create the structure of their contract themselves, within the limits of some very basic general rules such as:

(1) AGBG, Art 9 (Unfair Contract Terms Law): no contractual partner must be placed at an unreasonable disadvantage.
(2) BGB, Art 242: the parties must observe the rules of fairness and loyalty.
(3) GWB, Arts 15–18: the contract must not restrict competition and it must not prescribe prices or terms and conditions for third party contracts.
(4) GWB, Art 18: if the contract contains sole distribution rights and territorial protection clauses, it is subject to abuse control.

5.3.2 TERMS OF THE CONTRACT

Because of the lack of statutory regulations, franchise contracts should always be made in writing and contain at least the following essential provisions:

(1) A preamble in which the marketing concept of the franchisor is explained in detail.
(2) All commercial protective rights for which a licence is given to the franchisee should be listed separately.
(3) There should be a clear description of the contractual territory.
(4) The respective rights and obligations of the franchisor and franchisee should be clearly determined.

(5) Franchising fees should be included.
(6) The duration of the contract and termination procedure.
(7) Insurances.
(8) Cross supplies. Regulation of the possibility to purchase cross supplies from co-franchisees.

The above list is by no means complete. The legal position should always be checked carefully by a specialised solicitor before concluding a franchise contract.

5.3.3 TERMINATION

Hopefully the franchise contract itself will provide for ways and means of terminating the agreement. Existing gaps will have to be filled by general principles of law which apply to all long-term contracts. Every long-term contract can be terminated immediately, and without notice, if one party to the contract commits a serious breach of conditions (in the case of the franchisee, it could be a serious deviation from the franchise concept as agreed in the contract). Ordinary termination could possibly be determined in analogy to the law governing the termination of agency contracts, as there is a considerable similarity of interests. This would mean that six-week notice would have to be given.

Sometimes the courts have taken the view that the franchisee has the right to withdraw from the franchise contract under the provisions of the consumer protection law. This law provides a right of withdrawal from a contract for anybody who purchases goods and agrees to pay the purchase price in monthly instalments.

5.3.4 INDUSTRIAL PROPERTY PROTECTION FOR FRANCHISE SYSTEM?

The franchise system as a whole cannot be protected as an industrial property right because it does not constitute an invention or a design.

However, the individual elements which characterise the franchise concept such as the trademark for the franchise goods and the goods themselves (patent, if they constitute an invention) can be protected under the appropriate laws. (See Chapter 1.)

5.3.5 EEC LAW

A certain amount of restriction on competition is inherent in almost every franchising contract. Since most franchisors are working internationally, European competition law has to be taken into consideration when concluding a franchise contract. Such contracts often contain provisions which divide a country into distribution areas and prohibit the franchisees from expanding into other EEC member countries. Such clauses are in conflict with Art 85 of the Treaty of Rome. The European Commission has issued a group exemption ordinance number 4087–88 to deal with the restrictive effects of goods franchising. Other types of franchising (services franchising, know-how franchising) are subject to a number of different ordinances.

The basic position under EEC law can be summed up as follows:

(1) Conditions which are essential to protect the expertise of the franchisor are possible, even if they restrict competition.
(2) It is never considered essential for a franchisor to restrict the franchisee in his freedom to select his own customers.
(3) Territorial protection clauses are prohibited.
(4) Small and medium-sized franchise systems can be exempted from the above rules by virtue of the bagatelle ordinance if their overall market share is negligible.

EEC law, rather than German law, should therefore be considered when questions of distribution types arise.

5.4 OTHER FORMS OF DISTRIBUTION

A further form of distribution, which can be described as a hybrid variation of agency and franchising, is the so-called 'home trading system'.

5.4.1 HOME TRADERS

The 'home trader' (*Eigenhändler*) is an independent merchant who is closely integrated into the sales organisation of a major supplier by virtue of a skeleton contract. The skeleton contract outlines the general relationship between the home trader and his supplier. It imposes numerous duties on the trader, which serve to make him an integral part of the supplier's distribution system. Home traders are frequently encountered in the car trade where they are called appointed dealers.

The relationship between the home trader and the supplier

Large suppliers choose their home traders carefully in order to keep up a high standard of service in relation to the sale of their product. They will only appoint traders who are willing to satisfy a number of conditions:

Sole trader. Usually the home trader will have to promise to trade solely with the supplier's product. He will not be allowed to enter into a contractual relationship with a competing supplier — this is the reason why new VW cars and new Mercedes are never sold in the same garage. The sole trading duty is usually extended to spare parts as well.

Service. The trader will have to maintain a high standard of customer service, including a repair service. He will have to have well-trained personnel to deal with any queries his customers might have.

Presentation and advertising. Certain minimum standards for the presentation of the supplier's goods will have to be satisfied. For this purpose, the supplier will have the right to inspect the trader's premises. The trader will also have to make contractually prescribed efforts to advertise the goods.

Loyalty. Strict loyalty obligations apply to both parties because of the intensity of the contractual relationship.

Protection of the trader

Territorial protection. In return for the loss of his freedom to trade with a variety of different products, the home trader usually receives territorial protection. The supplier will guarantee to him that no other traders will be supplied with the same product within a certain contractually delineated area. This clause restricts competition and can therefore be declared void by the German Cartels' Authorities under certain circumstances (see Section **2.3**).

If the system affects the trade between EEC member states, EEC Law prohibits territorial protection clauses.

Supply. The furnishing of his stocks is naturally of great importance to the dealer. Therefore a separate 'warehouse contract' is often concluded to regulate this matter. The warehouse contract will establish the amount of the supplier's goods that the dealer will have to keep in store. It can also provide for the possibility to return unsold goods.

Compensation. In the event of termination of the contract, the trader is entitled to a compensation payment. Precedents have established that the law governing the compensation for trading agents can be applied to home trading contracts as well.

5.4.2 FOREIGN COMPANIES

In principle, foreign companies can set up branches in Germany without having to found a subsidiary German company, because they enjoy the same legal capacity in Germany as they have in their own country. However, German courts, unlike English courts, demand that the formation of the company has to comply with the law in force in the country of the seat of administration. This contrasts with the foundation principle, which allows companies to be founded in one state and have their seat elsewhere (this principle is applied by the British courts). As a result, German courts will refuse foreign companies, with their main seat in Germany, the right to set up branches, unless such companies are re-founded in accordance with the requirements of German law.

With the further progress of the agreement between all EEC member countries concerning the mutual recognition of companies and legal entities (which is not yet fully in force), these difficulties should soon cease to exist.

6
PROPERTY AND SUCCESSION

6.1 INTRODUCTION

The purpose of the following chapter is to give a brief outline of the types of property transactions which are likely to be encountered whilst setting up and running a business in Germany. Property can either be acquired contractually (*inter vivos*) or by virtue of succession. Like most laws, German property law distinguishes between movable and immovable objects (chattels and real estate). The transfer of ownership in movable objects can be completed immediately and, as a rule, no formalities have to be observed. On the other hand, the transfer of land and other immovable objects is strictly formalised and requires several steps for its successful completion.

The transfer of property by means of succession is governed by similar formal requirements, all of which serve to protect the position of the parties involved.

6.2 PROPERTY LAW

German property law is governed by the so-called 'doctrine of abstraction'. The transfer of property is perceived as an abstract transaction, which must not be confused with the promissory contract, in which the vendor and the purchaser agree on the sale of an object. The promissory contract does not transfer the property in the object to the buyer. It only constitutes a promise to convey such property in the future.

A second contract, the so-called 'abstract contract' is necessary to transfer the ownership in the goods sold. This abstract contract, which will usually be implied by an act of the vendor, has to be accompanied by a change in the possession of the goods. This last requirement is usually fulfilled by actual delivery of the goods to the purchaser. Other more sophisticated forms of transfer of possession are, however, recognised by the law as well.

6.2.1 SALE OF MOVABLE OBJECTS

For business purposes, the reader of this book can find himself in the position of a purchaser or a vendor of goods. To set up a business in Germany, he will have to purchase office equipment. He might also wish to sell his own product in Germany or indeed buy German products for export. A brief outline of an average purchase transaction will therefore be given below.

Promissory contract

As a first step, a promissory contract, which describes the quantity and quality of the goods concerned and fixes the purchase price and other rights and obligations of the parties, will have to be concluded. Once this contract has been signed, each party can sue the other for specific performance.

Transfer of ownership

The vendor is now bound by his promise to transfer the ownership of the goods to the purchaser. This is usually done by virtue of delivery of the goods. The delivery is viewed to contain the abstract declaration that the vendor herewith parts with his property and transfers it to the purchaser.

Often it will not be possible to physically hand over the goods sold. Sophisticated constructions serve to replace the performance of this act:

Article 931 of the Civil Code. Under this article, property and goods which are stored in the possession of a third party are handed over by means of an abstract contract, which transfers the vendor's right to demand delivery of the goods from the third party to the purchaser. To be valid, this document needs to give an accurate description of the goods sold which allows the third party to identify them beyond all reasonable doubt. For example, 'I herewith transfer my right to demand delivery of all boxes marked A which are stored in room 20 in the warehouse of . . .'.

Article 930 of the Civil Code. This article covers the transfer of property in goods which are to remain in the possession of the vendor. Such goods can be transferred immediately by drawing up an abstract contract declaring that the vendor agrees to hold those goods on the purchaser's behalf from a given date and further agrees to deliver them to whatever person the purchaser shall direct.

Purchase in good faith

Ownership in goods which do not belong to the vendor can be acquired by a purchaser in good faith with the notable exemption of stolen goods.

In the event of an ownership dispute, the purchaser will have to show that he was justified in believing that the vendor actually owned the goods in question. This task, though simple on the surface, can be full of legal traps for the unsuspecting businessman. He is expected to take into consideration that most large suppliers of goods operate with extensive bank credit, and might, therefore, have granted security rights or liens on their goods to a bank. Additionally, many vendors will refuse to complete the transfer of ownership before full payment of the purchase price. As a result, most products stored in shops and warehouses will probably belong to a supplier or a bank. These hidden owners will usually grant the vendor permission to sell the goods concerned within the due course of his business. It is, therefore, important to understand the network of security rights and reservations which is in use in Germany. All commercial purchasers and suppliers are expected to clarify the position regarding third party property rights. A statement on their existence and on the question of a permission to sell the goods in due course of business should always be obtained. If due inquiries have shown that no apparent obstacles exist to the transaction, the purchaser can rely on his good faith against claims brought by third parties.

6.2.2 REAL PROPERTY

Real property is defined as land and immovable objects which are inseparably attached to the land. Attached objects cannot be sold separately, unless it is possible to remove them from the land without thereby diminishing their value or the value of the land. A statutory exemption exists for property in flats. The basic rule of law regarding real property transactions is that the buyer acquires the land with all buildings and other constructions that are erected on it. Unless the contract otherwise specifies, the transfer is also deemed to include such movable objects as serve the purposes of the land (machines or other equipment belonging to business premises).

Purchase procedure

According to the principle of abstraction which governs German property law (see Section **6.1**), several separate steps are needed in order to complete the transfer of real property.

Purchase contract. As a first step, the parties will have to conclude a promissory contract in which the vendor promises to transfer a certain specified piece of land to the purchaser for monetary consideration. This promissory contract has to be drawn up and sealed by a notary public to be valid. It binds the parties for their future transactions but it does not yet transfer property in the real estate.

Intermediate period. Once the promissory contract has been concluded, the purchaser will usually pay the purchase price to the notary public who will deposit it in a fiduciary account. The notary will then proceed to obtain a copy of the relevant pages of the Land Registry and prepare a list of declarations of consent, which will need to be obtained before the transaction can be completed. These include the land transfer duty declaration, the declaration that the local city council will not exercise its statutory right of pre-emption and declarations of consent of mortgagors and other parties having a secured interest in the land.

If the land has been mortgaged, the parties can agree for the purchaser to maintain the mortgage. The vendor will have to reduce the purchase price in this event, and the consent of the mortgagor will have to be obtained. Other rights, such as easements, may have to be removed by the vendor if the purchaser does not agree to accept them.

Abstract contract. Once the notary has clarified all questions concerning the legal burdens and third party interests in the land, he can proceed to prepare a second notarial document, the so-called abstract contract (*Auflassung*). In this document, the vendor declares that he now transfers the ownership in the said piece of land to the buyer.

Registration. The abstract contract will also contain a clause empowering the notary public to apply for registration of the buyer as the new owner of the land. Registration is an essential requirement for all land transactions. Property in the land will not pass to the purchaser unless the registration procedure has been completed.

This procedure is lengthy since various official documents, such as the statement concerning land transfer duty and the statement concerning pre-emption rights, have to be produced before an entry is made by the registrar. To prevent the vendor from further dispositions concerning the piece of land, the purchaser will usually have a provisional notice of purchase entered into the registry. This notice will protect him against all subsequent registrations.

Functions of the Land Registry

The Land Registry is a public registry which is kept by a registrar at each court of first instance. German real estate has been fully registered since as early as 1897. Today each piece of land is described and numbered in the local registry. All current and previous owners, as well as all current and previous mortgagors, are listed in the Land Registry. The Land Registry enjoys great 'public confidence' which means that the correctness of all entries made into the register can be relied upon, without having to make further inquiries. As a result, it is possible to purchase a piece of land from the person who is registered as the proprietor, even if someone else is the true owner.

To interrupt with this process, the true owner can have an 'objection' entered into the register which will destroy the good faith of the purchaser and thereby protect the position of the true owner. The existence of an objection to ownership can make it virtually impossible for a proprietor to sell his land. Therefore, the law gives him the remedy of an injunction against wrongful objections. The entire issue can be further complicated by the registration of a provisional notice of purchase on behalf of a purchaser which serves to protect his position until the property is formally registered in his name. The documenting notary will usually give expert advice on the legal problems involved.

Mortgages

German law knows two different kinds of mortgages, the *Grundschuld* (free mortgage) and the *Hypothek* (accessory mortgage). Accessory mortgages can only be created to secure a specified right to a liquidated amount, whilst free mortgages can be used to secure unliquidated debts, such as overdraft facilities or variable credit arrangements. Germany has strict formal requirements for the creation of mortgages and failure to observe them renders the mortgage void. In order to be valid, the mortgage must be:

(1) contained in a notarial deed which describes the mortgaged property in full detail;
(2) registered in the Land Registry, and
(3) in the case of an accessory mortgage, it must also serve to secure a liquidated debt.

Proprietor's own mortgage. It is a peculiarity of German law that a mortgagee can acquire a mortgage on his own land. A proprietor's mortgage (*Eigentümergrundschuld*) is automatically created whenever a loan, which is secured by an accessory mortage, has been fully repaid. This principle, which may appear confusing at first sight, serves the very sensible purpose of securing the rank of a valuable first mortgage for renegotiation of interest rates with the second mortgagor.

Rights and remedies of a mortgagee. Once a secured loan has been repaid, the mortgagor loses his right to seize the property. In the case of an accessory mortgage, the position of the mortgagee is very well protected by the law. Free mortgages, on the other hand, will not expire automatically, and to terminate them, they must be removed from the register.

Leasehold interest

German law knows a limited number of registrable property rights. They are:

- Mortgages.
- Easements.
- Leasehold interests (*Erbbaurecht*).

While easements are of little interest to the businessman, a few words should be said about the German concept of leasehold interests. The creation of leasehold interests is perceived as a particularly beneficial way of financing the construction of a family home. Other than in the United Kingdom, leasehold interests are rarely sold as such on the market. Instead of purchasing the leasehold interests for a lump sum, the leaseholder will usually pay an annual 'fee' (*Zins*) similar to a rent to the owner of the freehold. The interest usually runs for 99 years with an option for the leaseholder to purchase the freehold at the end of the prescribed period. It must not be confused with another type of lease (*Miete*) which creates no interest in land.

6.2.3 CO-PROPERTY

If two persons acquire a piece of land together, they become joint owners of it and they will be registered in the Land Registry as holding co-property with one half share each.

Co-property can be sold or mortgaged separately but all transactions affecting the land as a whole, such as the erection of a building on the land, require consent of all the proprietors.

Property can also be shared by several persons as an indivisible whole. This is the case if two or more persons form a partnership for the purpose of acquiring property in real estate which they wish to use jointly. General and limited partnership companies normally own their business premises jointly. This form of co-property has the advantage that the property cannot be divided into individual shares. It is, therefore, impossible to introduce a new co-proprietor into the group without the consent of the other business partners. In this manner, property can be bound to a partnership company even though the partnership itself cannot own property because it is not a legal entity.

6.2.4 BUSINESS LEASES

Strictly speaking, the law governing business leases does not constitute part of the law of property under the German legal system. Leases are perceived as part of the law of contract, because they do not affect the ownership in real estate. Articles 535ff of the Civil Code apply to leases. A distinction has to be made between the lease of business premises (*Miete*) and business leases (*Pacht*). Business leases involve the right to make use of an entire factory or other business with all supplementary equipment for the agreed period. A lease of business premises simply involves the rent of rooms and land.

Leasing business premises

Leasing or, strictly speaking, renting business premises involves the conclusion of a contract which has to be made in writing, if it involves a renting period of one year or more. The main legal problem that has to be dealt with when drawing up a lease for business premises concerns the protection of the lessee from termination of the lease. Whilst leases for private habitation are very well protected by statutory law, German law neglects business leases in this respect. The law simply provides for two months' notice to be given for termination of the lease at the next quarter — either on 31 March, 30 June, 30 September or 31 December. This is a very short period of time considering the commercial importance of a business location for the constant flow of customers, and the expense of moving to new premises, and advertising the change of address. The contract for the lease should, therefore, contain additional provisions for the termination of the lease, which protect the position of the lessee.

Business leases

Special statutory provisions apply if an entire business including machines, other equipment and expertise is let out (*Pacht*).

In the case of *Pacht*, the responsibility for the upkeeping of the premises is shifted from the lessor to the lessee. He has to carry out the necessary repairs and replace damaged or outdated equipment. Upon termination of the lease, the business as a whole, inclusive of all old and new equipment, has to be returned to the lessor. Obviously, a lease of this kind requires sound protection for the lessee and his investments. The law provides for annual notice to be given, but longer terms can be agreed upon in the contract for the lease.

6.3 SUCCESSION

The main doctrine governing German law of succession is that of the freedom of each individual to dispose of his property according to his liking. However, this freedom is restricted by statutory law, which protects the immediate family of the deceased from being disinherited. Many of the complicated questions associated with the law of succession are of no particular relevance to the businessman. Therefore, only a basic outline of the general principles that govern succession will be described below.

6.3.1 TYPES OF SUCCESSION

Succession can be determined by will and other similar instruments, such as an inheritance contract, or by statutory law. Statutory law applies where wills are void or incomplete. It also limits and controls the power of the deceased to dispose of his property by naming certain obligatory heirs (*Pflichtteil*).

Statutory succession

If a person dies without leaving a will, the law provides for statutory succession. The law uses a parentage system which divides the relatives of the deceased into three orders. The first order consists of wife and children who receive equal shares and take priority over other relations. The second order is made up from the parents of the deceased and their descendents (brother, sister, niece etc) whilst the third order consists of the deceased's grandparents and their descendants. As a rule, descendants take priority over ascendants (parents, grandparents and their children) and if no descendants are alive, all ascendants and their children which are more than three times removed from the deceased, receive equal shares. Closer relations take priority over removed relations. Thus, if A dies a childless bachelor, but has two brothers and one aunt still living, his estate will be inherited by both brothers in equal shares.

Arbitrary succession

Wills. To be valid, a will needs to be either sealed by a notary public or handwritten by the deceased himself. Typed wills are void. It is important to note that the wife and children of the deceased cannot be disinherited by will. The law guarantees that they receive a statutory minimum inheritance (*Pflichtteil*) which is 50 per cent of what they would have received according to statutory law. Extraordinary gifts (houses, large sums of money) may also be called in question if their value exceeds the *Pflichtteil*. As a result, only childless bachelors can dispose of their wealth as they please.

The deceased can appoint a trustee or executor to manage the estate for a period of up to 30 years after his death. Longer appointments will be reduced to the maximum period.

Two-sided testament. Instead of a plain will, an inheritance contract or a two-sided testament can be concluded.

The two-sided testament is a type of will whereby married couples may each appoint the survivor as heir of their property. Often children are appointed as obligatory heirs to the survivor (*Berliner Testament*). After the death of one spouse, the two-sided testament becomes permanently binding on the survivor.

Inheritance contracts serve an altogether different purpose. They dispose of the testator's assets before his death by appointing somebody as heir in return for some consideration (usually services such as medical care). The appointment is binding but the *Pflichtteil* (see above) must be respected.

Business succession

If a businessman dies, the question arises of how to distribute his company between his heirs. He will usually seek to prevent the company from being torn apart or sold. In the case of legal entities (GmbH, AG), this is simply a matter of whom to leave the shares in the company to and how to compensate the other members of the family. The death of a partner in a general or limited partnership causes considerably more difficulty. The law assumes that the partners will not necessarily wish to accept all heirs of the deceased as new partners, because it cannot be foretold how these people will perform as businessmen. Furthermore, the size of the partnerships would grow out of proportion by means of succession. Therefore, two contractual and one so-called testamentary solution have been developed.

Contractual solutions. The partners can agree that the shares of the deceased will accrue to them, and that they will subsequently transfer those shares to the most suitable one amongst the heirs of the deceased.

Alternatively, the articles of association can name a limited number of potential successors, in which case, each of the partners will have to make sure that one of the persons named in the articles of association actually becomes his heir, or the whole concept fails.

Testamentary solution. Another solution is the so-called testamentary solution, which involves the appointment of a trustee who administers the partnership share of the deceased on behalf of his family for a prescribed period of time, which must not exceed 30 years. In the case of a general partnership, the trustee must, however, be willing to accept personal liability. Otherwise the partnership share of the deceased has to be transformed into the share of a limited partner. The Commercial Code provides a procedure for this transformation.

6.3.2 Inheritance Tax

Questions of inheritance tax play a major role in the area of succession. Whilst close relations are entitled to tax-free allowances (wife, children: DM 90,000 and grandchildren: DM 30,000 — 1991 figures) other heirs may have to part with up to 70 per cent of the inherited estate. Various constructions exist to avoid this. The early formation of a silent partnership or a limited partnership, between the testator and his heir, is a popular solution to this problem. However, nothing should be done without the advice of an experienced solicitor when dealing with such matters.

7
IMMIGRATION AND EMPLOYMENT

7.1 IMMIGRATION

Whilst most EEC nationals enjoy considerable freedom to move between EEC member countries and to work where they choose, the right of non-EEC nationals who intend to reside in Germany, are much more restricted.

7.1.1 NON-EEC NATIONALS

Most non-EEC nationals who intend to live in Germany on a permanent basis will need to apply for a residence permit as soon as they arrive at their destination (this rule includes American citizens, Canadians and Australians).

Some foreign nationals require a residence permit in the form of an entry visa before entering the country (this includes people from Turkey, Poland and Sri Lanka). Employment of a person who does not have a residence permit is a criminal offence. A comprehensive list of the rules which apply to nationals from different countries of the world can be found in the 'Foreigners Law' (*Ausländergesetz*) which is printed in the *Satorius* collection of administrative laws.

A working permit (*Arbeitserlaubnis*) is needed for non-EEC nationals wishing to work in Germany, unless their country is party to a bilateral working agreement (such as Austria, Sweden and Switzerland). Such permits are issued by the local department of employment (*Arbeitsamt*). Persons who have entered the country on a tourist visa will, as a rule, not be granted a residence or a working permit. It is advisable to check with the local administration authorities in advance whether a permit can be obtained or not.

7.1.2 EEC NATIONALS

Nationals of EEC member states have the right to receive a residence permit which may not be refused to them. They do not need to seek authorisation to work in Germany, unless they are members of certain professions for which a proof of sufficient qualification is required (eg, lawyers).

7.2 EMPLOYMENT LAW

German labour law consists of a confusing variety of different statutes. Plans to compile them into a single employment code have not yet been carried out. Therefore, the following main labour laws have to be distinguished.

(1) Individual employment law deals with the contractual relationship between an employer and a particular employee. It includes law of contract, and protective laws such as the law of termination protection.
(2) Business constitution law governs the internal organisation of large and medium-sized firms, including the right of co-determination and internal collective agreements.
(3) Collective bargaining law covers such matters as strikes, the formation of trade unions, and collective bargaining agreements.

The relationship between the various laws is hierarchical. The pyramid of employment laws is based upon the employment contract, which can be modified by collective agreements, which must in turn obey the rules of statutory law. Thus, the following order of priority applies:

(1) Binding rules of statutory laws and regulations.
(2) Collective bargaining agreements.
(3) Factory agreements.
(4) Internal collective agreements.
(5) Individual contract.

An exemption to this rule is contained in the so-called 'benefit principle' which allows agreements of a lower ranking to prevail if they are more beneficial for the employee than the collective agreement. Unfavourable divergences from higher ranking law are void, with certain exemptions in the case of collective bargaining agreements. The latter are perceived as containing an overall beneficial compromise.

7.2.1 EMPLOYMENT CONTRACTS

An employment contract must normally be concluded for an indefinite period of time. Fixed term contracts cannot be concluded unless special circumstances justify them. The Federal Labour Court has accepted the following justifications as sufficient:

(1) Need for temporary staff.
(2) Need to fulfil a specific task such as a research project.
(3) Seasonal jobs.
(4) Up to 18 months fixed term for a single contract under the employment promotion law.

Courts take a very strict view of these matters because fixed term contracts are often used by employers as means of avoiding the generous protection against termination that employees otherwise enjoy under German law. So-called chain contracts will, therefore, be treated as contracts for an indefinite period of time. The use of trial periods is, however, permitted.

Employees

Only true employees enjoy the protection of German labour law. So-called independent staff, who are paid for each piece of work separately, are not included in these rules. Judges and government officials have the status of a *Beamter* (civil servant) which is governed by public administrative law. For the purposes of this book, it is important to point out that managing directors and other high calibre white-collar staff do not fall into the category of an employee either. These persons represent the employer and exercise authority over the employees. As a result they cannot claim protection under labour law, and must seek to secure their position by virtue of contractual clauses.

Salary and social insurance

Basically, salaries can be contractually agreed upon by the employer and the employee. For most blue-collar workers and an increasing number of white-collar professionals, this rule is modified by minimum wages set out in collective bargaining agreements. These also contain minimum rates for the so-called flexible salary components, such as pay for overtime, night shift, dirty work, or dangerous work. The employer has to insure the employee and deduct income tax payments from his salary. Insurance and pension schemes vary according to the type of profession involved. Some employers set up their own insurance and pension schemes, whilst others join the official governmental insurance or a specialised insurance system set up by their professional body.

Full salary is payable for a period of up to six weeks of permanent illness. Thereafter, the relevant insurance will grant a daily sick pay. If the employee has been injured through the fault of a third party, both the employer and the insurance can recover their losses from that party. The employee is not entitled to sick pay if he has caused his illness by means of careless behaviour. Very controversial examples for this last rule can be found in the field of hazardous sports (hang-gliding, parachuting) and traffic accidents (not fastening a seat belt).

Employers who employ more than 15 workers must employ one handicapped person (6 per cent of employees). Employers who refuse to fulfil this obligation are subject to a special tax of DM 150 per month for each empty position.

Paid holidays

Usually a worker is entitled to 18 days' paid holiday, with minimum entitlements set out by collective bargaining agreements and statutory law (18 days' holiday are the statutory minimum). Over 15 bank holidays exist in Germany.

In the case of new employees, a six month waiting period has to elapse before the first holiday can be taken. Pregnant women are entitled to take four months' paid pregnancy leave and a further 12-month mother's leave during which time they receive a subsidised pay of DM 600 per month. An optional father's leave is also available.

Hazardous work

Some kind of work involves a particularly high probability of accidental damage to items of great value (for example, driving a truck or a caterpillar, operating a crane). As a rule, the employee cannot be held fully liable by his employer for damage which occurred in the course of such hazardous work, unless he is guilty of gross negligence. In cases of slight negligence, the cost of the damage is borne by the employer. It is usually split between the employer and employee in the event of so-called medium negligence. The doctrine of hazardous work is an unwritten rule of law which has been developed by the Federal Labour Court. It protects the employee from liabilities for damages which are unreasonably high in proportion to his income. The final apportionment of damages is left to the discretion of the court.

If the damage is done to third party property, the employer has an obligation to indemnify the employee against monies which have to be paid to the third party. Injuries suffered by colleagues at work are fully covered by the employer's general insurance.

7.2.2 TERMINATION

As a rule, a contract of employment is concluded for an unlimited period of time. While fixed term contracts end upon expiry of the agreed period, unlimited contracts have to be terminated by notice or by termination agreement.

Termination by notice

Most employment contracts are terminated by ordinary or by extraordinary notice. A notice must be worded clearly and unambiguously. When it has been received by the other parties, it is binding and cannot be rescinded. Many collective bargaining agreements provide for notice to be made in writing.

Ordinary notice. Most contracts for employment will be terminated by ordinary notice. Both parties must observe certain prescribed notice periods and termination dates in this event. Termination dates are fixed dates which must be used when calculating the notice period — for example, if the termination date is the end of a month, say September, and the notice period is 14 days, notice must be given 14 days before the end of September, therefore before 17 September.

The following paragraphs illustrate the statutory notice periods as set out by German labour law. The length depends on the profession of the employee and the duration of the employment contract.

The basic statutory notice period is two weeks to the end of the month for blue-collar workers and six weeks to the calendar quarter for white-collar workers (see Section **6.2.4**).

For workers with five years' service, the notice period is doubled and increases further after eight years' service for white-collar workers and after ten years' service for both blue and white-collar workers. The longest statutory periods are six months to the calendar quarter for white-collar workers with

12 years' service and three months to the end of the calendar quarter for blue-collar workers with 20 years' service.

The notice period may be altered by means of collective bargaining agreement. The distinction between blue and white-collar workers has met some constitutional doubts and might have to be abandoned in the future.

Extraordinary notice. Extraordinary notice can be given at any time and regardless of a notice period, if an important reason for the immediate termination of the contractual relationship exists. Only severe offences will usually be acceptable as important reasons for termination. Examples include theft and fraud, constant illness, accepting bribes, constant lateness and other repeated failures to fulfil contractual obligations. Minor offences can add up to constitute an important reason. Notice must be given within two weeks of gaining knowledge of the relevant facts, or the right to give extraordinary notice is forfeited. Often supplementary ordinary notice is given to protect the employer's provision in the event that the labour courts consider the extraordinary notice to be void.

Protection against unfair dismissal

Employers are by no means free to terminate a contract of employment according to their liking. The law concerning protection against unfair dismissal demands a 'social justification' for each notice given to an employee. The law applies to virtually all contracts with the exception of:

(1) Employees that have not yet spent six months with the firm.
(2) Part-time staff who work less than ten hours per week or 45 hours per month.
(3) Businesses which employ less than five employees.
(4) Managing directors.

The law contains a comprehensive list of social justifications for a dismissal which includes:

(1) Reasons rooted in the personal behaviour of the employee such as, lateness, rudeness, weak performance, disobedience or regular illnesses. Minor offences require one or two written warnings prior to notice being given.
(2) Urgent business requirements such as the closing down of a department, computerisation or financial difficulties such as lack of orders or high debt.

In the latter case the employer has to further justify the individual choices he made for dismissal by showing that an alternative occupation within the firm is impossible for the person dismissed, and that the social aspects were given adequate consideration when selecting the employee for dismissal.

A points system exists which helps the employer to make the correct social selections. Points are scored for:

- Age.
- Number of dependants.
- Duration of employment with the company.
- Qualifications.
- Chances to find new employment.

Thus, for example, a young bachelor must be chosen for dismissal prior to a married father of four, if neither of them has a better qualification.

Special protection. Some groups of workers receive special protection from dismissal, which usually takes the form of a consent requirement. The following list contains the most important groups of specially protected persons:

(1) The consent of a workers' council is needed to dismiss one of their members.

(2) The consent of the main welfare office is needed to dismiss a handicapped person.

(3) Pregnant mothers cannot be dismissed except in very exceptional cases.

(4) The dismissal of trainees and apprentices requires the approval of an educational committee at the local chambers of commerce.

Actions in the labour court. To obtain legal protection against a dismissal which does not comply with the above requirements, the employee must lodge a complaint to the labour court within three weeks of the date of notice. Once this period has expired, the employee loses his defence against the dismissal. If a complaint has been lodged, the case will often end with a compromise. For example, the contract is terminated, regardless of the validity of the notice, and the employee receives a tax-free compensation payment, which is calculated on the basis of his monthly salary multiplied by the years of employment with the firm (eg, with a salary of DM 12,000 and an employment of four years, the sum would be $4 \times 1{,}000 = 4{,}000$). Otherwise the employer is ordered to reemploy the employee or the claim is dismissed.

Each party bears their own costs before labour courts of first instance.

Termination of employment contract as a result of other events

Sale of business. The sale of a business to a new owner does not, in itself, constitute a viable social justification for the dismissal of an employee (Art 613(*a*) of the Civil Code).

However, in the course of restructuring the newly purchased company, urgent business requirements will often provide the necessary reasons for changes in personnel, such as the closure of a department.

Termination agreement. Employers sometimes seek to conclude private termination agreements with employees whom they wish to dismiss. The Federal Labour Court has taken a very strict view on the validity of such agreements. The employer will have to show that the employee signed the document in full knowledge of all his rights, especially the ones concerning protection against unfair dismissal. Otherwise, the court will not uphold the agreement.

7.2.3 EMPLOYEE CO-DETERMINATION

Two systems of co-determination rights for employees exist in Germany. Each company with more than five employees has an optional workers' council, which will deal with matters concerning the working conditions in the company. Furthermore, large GmbH and AG type companies also have to have employee representatives in their managing bodies.

The workers' council

Workers' councils are elected by all employees who are 18 years old or older. The size of the council depends on the number of employees. The employer must involve the workers' council in most of his routine decisions concerning the working conditions in his company including:

(1) Dismissal procedure — where consultation, but not consent is required before notice is given.
(2) Consent may be needed for the employment of new staff.
(3) The supervision of working conditions.
(4) Safety regulations.
(5) Co-determination in social matters such as meal breaks,

communal facilities, anniversary payments, and special rewards.

The workers' council has the power to conclude so-called factory agreements with the employer on behalf of the employees. This is a minor type of collective bargaining agreement, which regulates matters that fall within the sphere of responsibility of the workers' council. The agreements are binding on all employees of that particular company. Points which are usually dealt with in collective bargaining agreements cannot be the subject of a factory agreement. Social plans which provide for employee protection in cases of mass dismissal and bankruptcy are also devised by the workers' council. It has to be pointed out that all such agreements are contracts and must, therefore, comply with higher ranking statutory law.

Co-determination on the management level

Large companies can be subject to various degrees of employee co-determination on the management level. Employee representatives can be found in both the supervisory board (up to 50 per cent employees) and the board of directors (one employee *Arbeitsdirektor*). Companies of different sizes and types are affected as follows:

(1) For companies with over 500 employees, there are no employee representatives on the board of directors but they do form one third of the supervisory board.

(2) For steel companies with over 1,000 employees, employees have one representative on the board of directors and form half of the supervisory board, which also has one neutral representative who has the casting vote.

(3) For companies with over 2,000 employees, employees have one representative on the board of directors and form half of the supervisory board. In the event of a tie, the chairman, who is chosen by the shareholders, has a casting vote.

All other companies, in particular partnerships (KG, oHG) are exempt from this type of co-determination as are all immediate financial decisions by the board in all types of companies.

7.2.4 TRADE UNIONS AND COLLECTIVE BARGAINING

In Germany, the co-operation between trade unions and employers has constantly increased over the last decade. Collective bargaining agreements have long ceased to be the forum for a class struggle in Germany. Violent strikes and picketing have become rare and many collective bargaining agreements are renewed peacefully. So-called framework agreements (*Manteltarif*) contain important rules on the reciprocal rights of the parties which often replace statutory law. Additional short-term collective bargaining agreements deal with wage and salary questions (*Einzeltarif*).

Area of application

Initially, only those employees who were members of trade unions were bound by collective bargaining agreements. However, the Federal Employment Minister now has the power to give the force of law to collective bargaining agreements. Furthermore, it is possible to agree by means of individual contract that a certain collective bargaining agreement shall apply to that contract. Unreasonable references will, however, be disregarded by the court.

Priority rules

A collective bargaining agreement is binding on those to whom it applies by virtue of one of the above rules. Generally, contractual clauses which deviate from a collective bargaining agreement are void unless they serve to improve the position of the employee (the benefit principle). Rights arising from mandatory agreements can, however, be forfeited by the employee. Relatively short time limits (3–6 months) usually apply for collectively agreed employees' rights. If the employee has not brought any claims within the prescribed period, he normally loses his rights.

Strikes

The strike is the main weapon which trade unions can use to threaten employers. A strike paralyses the contract of employment, and the rule 'no work — no pay' applies. Strikes for other than bargaining purposes are illegal. This includes wildcat strikes which have not been called by trade unions, political strikes and sympathy strikes.

Lock-out

Whilst a strike has always been considered a legitimate weapon of the employee, the lock-out as the weapon of the employer is greatly disputed in Germany. The refusal to pay wages is perceived by many as a sufficient means for exerting pressure on the employees. In spite of this view, the Federal Labour Court has decided that a defensive lock-out may occasionally be justified.

7.2.5 DISCRIMINATION

Discriminative employment practice is prohibited by virtue of Art 3 of the German Constitution. Accordingly, nobody must be discriminated against as a result of his sex, race, origin, creed or religious and political views. Collective bargaining agreements and statutory law are directly bound by this principle.

The individual employer must also not discriminate against certain groups of employees. The doctrine of equal treament demands that arbitrary differences in treatment of employees are to be avoided. Article 611 (*a*) gives an action for damages against an employer who discriminates against employees because of their sex. Discrimination on account of other grounds can occasionally lead to claims for equal treatment.

7.2.6 LABOUR COURTS

In Germany, legal disputes concerning labour law have to be brought before special labour courts (see the introduction to this book). Professional and honorary judges sit together in labour cases. The honorary judges are appointed upon nomination by trade unions and employers' unions.

The procedural requirements are more relaxed and informal in the labour courts. The judges are expected to help the parties who are not legally represented with their case, and provide them with the necessary guidance. Costs are low and cannot be recovered from the losing party. Conciliatory proceedings, in which an attempt for amicable settlement has to be made, precede a trial.

8
TAXATION LAW

8.1 Introduction

In Germany, the right to levy taxes is held by both the federal government and the individual states. Furthermore, each city council can invent local taxes that bear direct reference to the local community, such as dog tax, horse tax or holiday home tax.

Foreigners are only affected by the obligation to pay German tax if they:

(1) live in Germany for more than six months;
(2) become permanently resident in Germany;
(3) earn income from German sources; or
(4) have German assets.

Double taxation agreements exist with:

Argentina	Iceland	Morocco
Australia	India	Netherlands
Austria	Indonesia	New Zealand
Belgium	Iran	Norway
Brazil	Ireland	Pakistan
Bulgaria	Israel	Philippines
Canada	Italy	Poland
China	Ivory Coast	Portugal
Cyprus	Jamaica	Romania
Czechoslovakia	Japan	Singapore
Denmark	Kenya	South Africa
Egypt	Korea	Soviet Union
Ecuador	Kuwait	Spain
Finland	Liberia	Sri Lanka
France	Luxembourg	Sweden
Great Britain	Malaysia	Switzerland
Greece	Malta	Thailand
Hungary	Mauritius	Trinidad and Tobago

Tunisia	USA	Zambia
Turkey	Yugoslavia	Zimbabwe
Uruguay		

The new federal states which were formerly part of the GDR are treated as part of the Federal Republic of Germany as from 1991. A solidarity tax is currently levied on their behalf in the former West Germany.

The German fiscal authorities have separate offices and their own police squad which investigates tax criminality. Most businesses are subjected to tax investigations every 2–5 years depending on their size. Documents can be impounded and taken away and interrogations can take place. Accurate bookkeeping is very important. Vouchers need to be kept to support deduction claims. Entertaining is only deductible up to a rather limited amount.

Appeals can be made against all decisions by the tax authorities. A separate set of courts (finance courts) with three instances exists to deal with fiscal disputes.

8.2 DIRECT TAXES

8.2.1 INCOME TAX

All persons who live in Germany are subject to a tax on their annual worldwide income, although double taxation agreements protect foreign income (see the list above). The nationality of those persons is irrelevant. Persons who reside elsewhere only have to pay tax on their domestic income. Legal persons (AG, GmbH) are subject to corporation tax. Partnerships neither pay income tax nor corporation tax, income tax being collected from all partners instead.

German tax law knows seven different sources of income:

(1) Wage and salary income, earned by employed workers.
(2) Income earned in agriculture and forestry.
(3) Trading income, earned by sole traders and partners.
(4) Income from capital, such as investment profits.
(5) Professional earnings gained by doctors, lawyers etc.
(6) Income from renting and leasing.
(7) Other income such as pensions, speculation profits and compensation payments.

Calculation of income tax

The earnings of each tax payer in a calendar year are totalled. Losses arising under one source of income can be set off against profits from another source. Further deductions can be made for special expenditures, which were necessary to maintain a positive income, such as the cost of travelling to work every day and for working equipment.

Table 8.1 Income tax

(1)	Mr Schult earns a salary of:	+	DM	30,000
(2)	Partner in a company:	–	DM	10,000
(3)	10 per cent interest on invested monies:	+	DM	1,000
(4)	Letting a room in his house:	+	DM	6,000
(5)	Veteran's pension:	+	DM	10,000
(6)	Train ticket for travelling to work:	–	DM	1,500
(7)	Total taxable income:		DM	35,500

Tax rates are progressive, commencing with a rate of 19 per cent and thereafter progressing until the maximum rate of 53 per cent is reached (for an income of DM 120,000 and more).

Married couples enjoy the benefit of joint assessment. This is particularly attractive if a discrepancy of income exists between husband and wife, because the income of both spouses is added together and then halved, thus lowering the overall tax rate. For instance, a single person earning DM 100,000 per annum will pay DM 30,743 tax, but a married couple jointly earning the same amount, and making use of joint assessment, will pay DM 22,168 tax only, thus saving DM 8,575.

Procedure

Whilst income tax is automatically deducted from salaries by the employer, self-employed persons will need to submit an income tax declaration by 31 May of each year. An estimate of the expected annual income is made by the fiscal authorities in the case of spouse employed persons. On the basis of this estimate, quarterly payments of income tax are collected. After the final annual assessment has been completed, excess payments are refunded. If the estimate was too low, additional tax is collected.

Income tax declarations for businesses should be prepared by a *Steuerberater* (chartered accountant) because of the complexity of German income tax law.

8.2.2 CORPORATION TAX

Profits made by corporations such as AG, GmbH and eG or VVaG (see Chapter 4) are subject to corporation tax at a flat rate of 50 per cent rather than income tax.

The tax which has been paid by the corporation is fully credited to the individual shareholders, thus avoiding double taxation. For these purposes, the law differentiates between two types of profits:

(1) Profits which are kept by the corporation are subject to the full rate of 50 per cent.

(2) Profits which are distributed immediately are subject to a reduced rate of 36 per cent.

The corporation tax is fully credited to the individual shareholder who will only need to pay the difference between his personal tax rate and the corporation tax. Non-resident shareholders will not be given credit for corporation tax, as they are not subject to German income tax.

One disadvantage of this system is the high tax burden for small corporations (50 per cent). Necessary company investments are, therefore, often made by means of the so-called 'dividend cash-back' procedure. Profits which are initially distributed as dividends to the shareholders at a reduced tax rate of 36 per cent are reimbursed to the company by the shareholders. The company can now proceed to invest the money without having to pay full corporation tax of 50 per cent.

Table 8.2 Corporation tax

Corporation

Profit	200				
Dividend	100	Tax	36%	Paid	64
Retained	100	Tax	50%	Tax	50

Shareholder with a high income tax rate of 53 per cent

Income	64		
Tax credit	36		
Total	100	Tax	53%
Income after tax	47		

Shareholder with low tax rate of 20 per cent

Income	64		
Tax credit	36		
Total	100	Tax	20%
Tax refund	16		
Income	80		

Deductions

As a rule, company expenses reduce the profit and are therefore deductible. However, some exemptions exist to this rule:

(1) Salary payments to members of the supervisory board can only be deducted at a rate of 50 per cent.
(2) Fines imposed by courts cannot be deducted.
(3) VAT for own use cannot be deducted (see Section **8.3.1**).

Moving to a foreign country

If a corporation moves its headquarters to a foreign country, all silent reserves have to be uncovered. Corporation tax at a rate of 50 per cent has to be paid on the difference between the lower balance sheet value and the higher true market value of all company assets (known as silent reserves). This provision serves to ensure that all profits are taxed at some point in time.

8.2.3 CAPITAL TAX

Capital tax is a periodic tax, which is levied on investments such as property, real estate, company shares, and interest-bearing monies. The tax rate is 0.5 per cent for natural persons and 0.6 per cent for corporations.

The tax is designed to collect a part of the assumed annual capital growth. However, if there was no growth, the substance of the property is affected by the tax as well. This has led to suggestions that capital tax ought to be abolished because it hinders investment and economic growth.

Calculation

There are relatively high tax-free allowances for natural persons:

- Any person: DM 70,000
- Married Couples: DM 140,000
- Each child: DM 70,000

Companies have lower allowances (for an AG the allowance is DM 20,000). The taxable value of real estate is based on the so-called 'unit value', which has last been fixed over 30 years ago and is therefore very low. The unit value does not reflect the true value of real estate.

Families can opt for joint assessment of parents and children.

Double taxation

Double taxation occurs in the case of capital tax. Both the corporation and its shareholders have to pay capital tax on their assets. If an individual shareholder exceeds his tax free allowance he will, therefore, be subject to double taxation.

8.2.4 INHERITANCE TAX

Gifts and inheritances are taxed very heavily in Germany, if they exceed a certain tax free allowance. The tax becomes due upon the accrual of an inheritance to a particular person. Inheritance tax is also payable every 30 years on the assets of a family foundation.

Rates

There are four tax classes, the tax rate is progressive and depends on the classification.

- Class 1: Spouse, children; 3–35 per cent.
- Class 2: Grandchildren, great grandchildren, parents, grandparents; 6–50 per cent.
- Class 3: Brothers, sisters and their descendants, relations by marriage, divorced spouses; 11–65 per cent.
- Class 4: Everybody else, in particular all legal entities; 20–70 per cent.

Allowances

Close relations can claim the following tax free allowances:

Spouses:	DM 250,000
Children:	DM 90,000
Grandchildren:	DM 50,000
Class 3:	DM 10,000
Class 4:	DM 3,000

Consecutive acquisitions which are accrued from the same donor within a period of ten years are added up for the purpose of calculating the allowances.

Procedure

The local tax office has to be notified of all taxable acquisitions within a period of three months. Failure to notify can result in criminal prosecution. Notaries and other officials are under an obligation to notify the tax authorities of any gifts or testaments which have been sealed in their office.

8.2.5 TRADE TAX

The object of trade tax is to collect a share of the trade earnings of all commercially active businesses for the public coffers. This is achieved by taxing both the earnings and the trade capital of the businesses concerned, according to a rather complicated method (*Gewerbeertragsteuer* and *Gewerbekapital-steuer*).

The basis for the assessment of trade tax is a standard figure which is applied to the trade earnings and the trade capital of each company. The amount of trade tax due is calculated from the resulting figure.

This basic figure is multiplied by the so-called 'tax levy rate', which is set by the local authorities and can vary considerably from town to town. Therefore, it is very important for anyone who wishes to set up a business in Germany to find out the levy rate which applies in a particular area. Some towns are known as 'tax paradises', having a very low levy rate for trade tax. Big investors sometimes have methods of convincing a city council to lower levy rates.

For this and other reasons, considerable efforts are under way to eliminate trade tax and capital tax, which are both perceived as obstacles to investment and economic growth. As a result trade tax is not levied in the territories of the former GDR.

8.3 INDIRECT TAXES

Indirect taxes are conceived to collect money from the consumer. For practical and political reasons, they are levied from the businesses which perform the taxable transaction with the consumer. It would be practically impossible to keep trace of the taxable transactions that a single consumer makes, and new direct taxes, such as income tax, will always meet with more political opposition than indirect taxes which are not felt immediately. Sometimes the tax burden is not passed on to the consumer by the businessmen, in which case the indirect tax has failed to achieve its object. This phenomenon was recently experienced in the United Kingdom when thousands of businesses did not pass the VAT increase from 15 per cent to 17.5 per cent on to the consumer.

8.3.1 VALUE ADDED TAX

Value added tax is the classic indirect tax that most European governments collect on consumption processes.

Tax payer

VAT is usually collected from businesses, though private individuals may occasionally be subject to import duty, which is a form of value added tax.

Anybody who carries out a commercial activity or charges VAT in an invoice for goods or services, is under an obligation to pay value added tax. This includes self-employed professionals, as well as farmers, landlords and of course all companies.

Taxable transactions

VAT is levied on all commercial sales transactions, and is also chargeable for services. Supplies for own consumption can also be taxed, but a large number of exemptions exists in this area. The leasing and renting of real estate is generally exempted from VAT.

The current rate is 14 per cent. A reduced rate of 7 per cent applies to certain privileged goods such as:

- Agricultural products.
- Foodstuffs.
- Certain drinks.
- Artistic creations.
- Fodder and fertilisers.
- Goods and services for own consumption.

A special rate of 11 per cent applies to certain agricultural transactions. Tax privileges concerning own supplies and services exist for small-sized companies.

Procedure

The individual businessman charges 14 per cent VAT as a separate item in his invoices, thus passing the tax burden on to the consumer. However, he is the tax debtor. As a rule, if he fails to collect VAT from his customers, he will still be liable to pay VAT to the fiscal authorities. VAT is collected from all businesses annually. As the amount of VAT due depends on the amount of taxable transactions performed in a year, the company must submit a tax declaration to the fiscal authorities, in which the amount of VAT which has been collected from the consumer must be calculated. VAT which has been paid to third parties can be deducted from this amount, if the tax debtor is a wholesaling or similar business.

Monthly advance payments. VAT calculations have to be submitted on a monthly basis and corresponding monthly advance payments have to be made. The tax authorities have the right to inspect the documents on which such payments and calculations are based at any stage.

Deductions. The company deducts all VAT which has been paid to third parties from the VAT which has accrued on sales in each monthly declaration. Only the surplus amount is collected by the tax office, because the business is not meant to carry the true tax burden, which is supposed to be passed on to the consumer who cannot deduct VAT from his tax bill.

Example

X sells goods for: DM 100,000
14% VAT thereon: DM 14,000
X buys goods for: DM 50,000
He is invoiced 14%
VAT by the vendor: DM 7,000
VAT due (14,000–7,000) = 7,000

If no surplus appears, a tax refund can be claimed.

Annual declaration. The final assessment of VAT is carried out at the end of the year. An annual tax declaration, showing all taxable transactions which have been completed in the last year, has to be submitted. Corrections can now be made for transactions which were cancelled, altered or delayed. Excess payments are refunded or set off against the last tax bill.

8.3.2 OTHER INDIRECT TAXES

Various minor indirect taxes exist in Germany, the most important ones of which are:

- Alcohol tax on spirits.
- Beer tax.
- Tobacco tax.
- Amusement tax.

and certain local taxes such as:

- Dogs tax.
- Horse tax.
- Holiday home tax.

which are levied locally by the city councils.

8.3.3 SPECIAL CONTRIBUTIONS

Germany knows yet another form of tax which is called a 'special contribution payment', because it is not a proper tax in the constitutional sense.

Special contributions are payments which have to be made by certain groups of businesses, which by the nature of their activities cause special public expense. For example, most water polluters have to pay special pollution contributions, which are calculated with reference to the amount of pollutants which have been emitted by the company during the last year.

Businesses with more than 15 employees, who refuse to employ their allotted number of handicapped people, have to pay a special contribution for handicapped people. This contribution amounts to 150 DM per month for each handicapped person allotted but not employed.

The monies which are received as special contributions have to be used to meet the special costs which are caused by the taxpayers. Thus pollution contributions have to be used for purposes of cleaning up rivers, while handicapped people's contributions have to be used for purposes of training handicapped people.

9
ENVIRONMENTAL AND PLANNING LAW

9.1 INTRODUCTION

German environmental and planning law forms part of the broad field of public administration, unlike the issues that have been covered so far which are concerned with civil law. While civil law is governed by contracts made between parties of equal standing, public administrative law is concerned with the relationship of a private individual or company to the state, and it is characterised by the subordination of the individual. As a result, applications and appeals rather than agreements prevail. The administration issues official orders, which the individual has to obey. He cannot choose to disobey an order because he is of the opinion that the order is not correct. Incorrect orders are enforceable unless objections are raised against them.

Some basic principles of German public law are outlined below.

9.2 BASIC GERMAN PUBLIC LAW

9.2.1 ADMINISTRATIVE STRUCTURES

The structure of the German administration is complicated and confusing. Federal offices and regional offices, which are subdivided into various smaller units, exist and have overlapping responsibilities. It is very important to direct applications to the correct office and it is equally important to know to whom to appeal against incorrect orders made by public authorities. As a rule, the first appeal must be made to the direct superior of the office which has made the decision. This will often be the *Regierungspräsident* (regional president) but it can also be the local mayor or a special officer. The appeal has to be submitted in writing within one month after receipt of the order.

Further appeals against their decisions can be made to the administrative courts, which are divided into three instances. The Federal Administrative Court in Berlin has the final say on all points of law of national importance.

9.2.2 ADMINISTRATIVE ORDERS

Administrative Orders are official documents in which permissions are granted or refused. Orders can also prohibit, restrict or redefine individual rights. Prohibitions and permissions are the most important administrative acts.

Permissions must be obtained in order to lawfully pursue certain activities. These include a trading licence before opening a business, a food and liquor licence for restaurants and bars, a building permit for the erection or alteration of a building, and various other permits for the operation of dangerous plants or health-related trades. Permits need to be applied for, often on prescribed forms. If the permission is refused, an appeal has to be made in writing, showing why the applicant believes that he is entitled to a permission.

Prohibitive orders are used to interfere with illegal or dangerous activities. Trading or building without permit will be prohibited and the order will usually be enforced immediately. Appeals can be made asking for the status quo to be restored.

9.2.3 FEDERAL AND NON-FEDERAL LAWS

The subject of German administrative law is further complicated by the distinction which is made between federal law and the law of the individual states. According to the German constitution, the Federal Parliament must not regulate subject matters which fall within an area of responsibility which has been reserved for the states. The distinction can be rather subtle, allowing the Federation to deal with one part of a matter whilst reserving another part of the same matter to the individual states. As a result, legislation often varies regionally, as do internal directives on the implementation of such laws. Thus, building law is contained in two different codes, the Federal Building Code and the Building Ordinances of the individual states. For practical purposes it is, however, sufficient to note that both laws will ultimately be applied by the same public office.

9.3 BUILDING LAW

German building law exists at all levels of administration.

- Federal law — Building Code.
- State law — Building Ordinances.
- Regional planning — Regional development plans.
- Local law — Local building plans.

The day-to-day matters of building law are set out in detail in local building plans, which are devised by the local council in accordance with the regional development plans. Such plans contain maps and drawings which determine the type and size of building which is permissible in a particular area. Exemptions from the rules of such plans can be granted under special circumstances, which are set out in the Federal Building Law which lists various types of building areas. The building ordinances of the individual states are concerned with the safety standards which have to be obeyed. Finally, unplanned areas exist, mainly in rural parts of the country, where building permission can only be granted if the proposed project fits into the environment (Federal Building Law, Arts 29–36).

9.3.1 BUILDING AREAS

Finding a suitable site for commercial businesses can be difficult because they can only be set up in certain designated areas, which are usually specified in a local building plan. These areas are called industrial areas. Mixed areas exist, in which 'clean' businesses of a certain kind can be allowed (eg, office buildings, shops). No businesses are allowed in pure residential areas.

Anybody has the right to inspect the local building plans to inform himself about the availability of suitable locations.

Once a building site has been found, a *Bauvoranfrage* should be made. This is an official enquiry as to the permissibility of a certain type of building on a particular lot. A positive answer is binding on the administration.

9.3.2 BUILDING ORDINANCE

The exact plans for a building project will be scrutinised as to their compliance with certain safety standards, which are set out in the building ordinance (including fire-safety, noise and hygiene).

Furthermore, demands concerning the creation of parking space, green areas or playgrounds can be made by the local authorities by virtue of the building ordinance.

9.3.3 NEIGHBOUR RIGHTS

Neighbours who are directly affected by a particular building project have the right to appeal against building permissions which have been granted for adjacent land. To succeed, they will have to show that their property will suffer severe disadvantages as a result of the project. If possible, the written consent of all neighbours should be obtained before commencing to build.

9.3.4 PROCEDURE

A building application has to be submitted. It needs to contain:

(1) The architectural plans.
(2) Proof that the plans were drawn up by a qualified architect or engineer.
(3) Drawings of the building.
(4) The name and address of the person building it.

If building permission is refused or granted with intolerable restrictions, an appeal can be made to the *Regierungspräsident*. Connection to public sewers, waste water systems, roads and other services is obligatory. A substantial connection fee can be charged.

9.3.5 LARGE PROJECTS

Building projects of commercial character can conflict with a number of laws and ordinances, such as anti-pollution laws, water and waste laws. Separate permissions need to be obtained for the project in this event. To simplify the procedure large projects such as factories, refineries or power stations will be dealt with in an all encompassing administrative procedure (*Planfeststellungsbeschluss*). This procedure leads to a final decision on the entire project, which is binding on all parties concerned. Neighbours are given the opportunity to voice their objections in a public meeting. Late objections are precluded.

9.4 ENVIRONMENTAL PROTECTION

A specialised law deals with the combat of pollution and the protection of the environment from nuisance and damage (BImSchG). Almost every commercial business will cause a noise nuisance (in the case of white-collar offices the nuisance may be caused by the arrival and the departure of the employees). Factories and industrial businesses will emit dust or chemical substances, and will also produce industrial waste. The relevant German laws submit all major projects to a complicated licensing procedure.

9.4.1 LICENSING

A specialised pollution ordinance contains an extensive catalogue of factories and plants which require a licence. Two classes of licensing, which depend on the type of plant involved, exist: simplified and formalised licensing.

Formalised procedure

The formalised procedure commences with an application for a licence, which is followed by the publication of the industrial project. All interested parties may now submit objections which have to be taken into consideration by the licensing authorities when reaching their decision.

Simplified procedure

The simplified procedure avoids the publication of the project, and is only available for smaller projects. Neighbours and other third parties will not be heard. They must appeal against the licensing decision, if they wish to object.

Licensing requirements

As a rule, plants have to be operated in such a way that harmful effects on the environment are avoided. Emissions have to be limited to a prescribed maximum amount. Special preventive measures, such as the installation of modern filters or water coolers, must be taken. If no methods exist to reduce the nuisance to an acceptable minimum, the licence will not be granted. German courts define the maximum values in accordance with certain officially approved technical instructions (TA Luft, TA Lärm). It is therefore advisable to show that the requirements set out by those instructions can be observed by means of suitable precautions, before submitting a licensing application. A special federal ordinance fixes maximum values for permissible chemical emissions.

Partial licences

If the basic requirements for a licence have been met, a partial licence can be granted. Partial licences contain a permission to build certain specified parts of a project. However, if it becomes apparent later on that a licence for the remaining parts cannot be granted, complicated problems occur. Large amounts of money which have already been spent will often make it politically difficult for the administration to refuse the permission for completion of the project, although pressure from environmental groups has led to the existence of several ghost plants which were never completed.

9.4.2 CONTROL OF UNLICENSED BUSINESSES

Businesses which do not require a licence, such as most shops and food retailers, are subject to supervision. If they become a nuisance, they can be closed down or required to reduce noise levels or other emissions.

9.5 WATER AND WASTE LAW

9.5.1 WATER LAW

Water laws aim to protect water as a natural resource by regulating its use. Large businesses will often need to use rivers or other public waters for commercial purposes (for example, cooling water for power plants and the emission of dirty water into rivers).

Certain uses of water are subject to licensing:

(1) Abstraction of water.
(2) The introduction of substances into water.
(3) The emission of substances into coastal waters.

Licensing

Licences for the introduction of substances into water are subject to stringent limits in Germany, which often forces large companies to operate their own sewerage plants to avoid exceeding their limits. Unlicensed pollution is punished by means of heavy fines.

Individuals responsible for such pollution commit a criminal offence. Article 22 of the Federal Water Law imposes a strict civil liability on all companies and individuals involved.

Licences can be revoked if maximum allowances for pollution, prescribed in the licence, are exceeded frequently.

9.5.2 WASTE DISPOSAL LAW

Waste is a hazard to health and an increasing environmental problem. Various laws deal with the disposal of waste, which can be classified into general waste and hazardous waste. General waste includes household refuse, glass bottles and print and paper and is covered by the General Waste Law. Hazardous waste includes nuclear fuel, chemical waste and animal carcasses and is covered by special waste laws.

As a rule all non-hazardous waste is dealt with by local authorities. They are obliged to arrange regular waste collections and recycling and disposal of the collected items. The disposal of hazardous wastes is dealt with by the individual *Länder*.

Private waste disposal

Big plants and factories, which produce large amounts of waste, can be required to provide for their own system of waste disposal. Some companies prefer to export their waste to foreign countries where environmental protection laws are less strict. According to Art 2 of the German Waste Law, they require a licence for waste export, in an attempt to restrict 'waste tourism'. However, EEC waste directives demand the freedom to export waste within the community without restrictions. The licensing requirements in Germany are, therefore, in need of change.

9.6 ENVIRONMENTAL LIABILITY LAW

On 1 June 1991 a new environmental liability law came into force in Germany. It is designed to encourage companies which operate hazardous plants to develop safer production processes by imposing a strict liability for damage to the environment on them.

9.6.1 Hazardous Plants

The law lists 96 types of hazardous plants, including plants from the following fields of industry and commerce:

- Mineral oil.
- Heat generation.
- Power companies.
- Chemicals.
- Pharmaceutical companies.
- Ceramics.
- Waste recycling plants.

The erection of hazardous plants is subject to a licensing procedure according to the Environmental Protection Law (see Section **9.4.1**).

Plants which have been shut down, or which are still under construction, are included in the definition of a hazardous plant, as well as movable technical equipment and machines.

9.6.2 Liability

German law has always known a liability based on fault. This principle has recently been supplemented by various strict liability laws:

(1) Products liability law.
(2) Medical products liability law.
(3) Road Traffic Act.
(4) Environmental liability law.

The justification for strict liability is derived from the fact that the production or operation of hazardous items is in itself dangerous. People who wish to make use of hazardous objects must, therefore, bear the consequences.

As a result, the new Environmental Liability Law applies regardless of fault. Mere causation of damage is sufficient to give rise to liability. But the law goes even further, as it also assumes causation, if a particular type of plant is generally capable of causing the kind of damage which has occurred. The claimant only needs to show that the causation took an ‘environmental path’ — namely progressed via such media as water or soil. This provision is intended to cover instances where chemicals cannot be traced back to their origins. In such cases, the potentially responsible plants will now have to show that they did not cause the damage.

Environmental damage

As a rule, all damage which has been caused to the environment is covered by the law. This includes unforeseeable damage, such as damage resulting from the release of substances, the dangerous effect of which had not been recognised before their release. However, in the latter case full proof of causation is required to establish liability.

Limitation of liability

Liability is excluded in the event of Acts of God. These are defined to include natural events such as storms and floods as well as external interferences such as acts of sabotage and strikes.

The global maximum liability is DM 160 million. Each individual victim can be awarded up to DM 50,000 per annum. Obligatory insurance has to be obtained by all operators of hazardous plants to cover potential claims for environmental damage.

EEC law

The European Commission has produced a draft proposal concerning liability for industrial waste. The proposal overlaps to a surprisingly large extent with German law, because it defines waste in the widest possible sense. All objects which are disposed of by their owners are defined as waste. If the proposal is successful, EEC law might take priority over German law to a certain extent.

9.7 PRODUCT LABELLING

Product labelling is governed by a variety of specialised laws and ordinances. Each regulation deals with a certain kind of product. The most important law is the law concerning foodstuffs and utility articles, which covers tobacco, toys, cosmetics, cleaning agents and clothes.

9.7.1 FOODSTUFFS

The law contains a ban on the use of prohibited additives in foodstuffs, which are listed in various ordinances. Permitted additives and radiation may be used, but their use must be revealed to the consumer on the product label. Phrases such as 'salt, sugar and artificial additives contained' do not suffice. All ingredients must be clearly spelt out in detail on the label.

Additionally, certain fresh foods such as milk or cheese may only be sold in containers of a prescribed type. On the container the following details must be given:

(1) The time of production.
(2) The time of packaging.
(3) The date by which the product should be consumed.
(4) Details of origin and preparation.

It is a criminal offence to make misrepresentations on labels and the sale of foods after the expiry date is prohibited.

9.7.2 COSMETICS

Cosmetics must also be labelled in great detail. Ingredients, date of production, and expiry dates must be listed, as well as the name and the address of the manufacturing company. Instructions for use and warnings about risks and dangers must also be given, either on the container itself or on a separate leaflet inside the packaging.

9.7.3 EEC LAW

Overall, German law is very restrictive as far as admissible additives to products are concerned. Many regulations are, therefore, in conflict with the free movement of goods within the European community. A well-publicised example of this conflict concerns recent dispute concerning the German purity laws for beer brewers. These laws prohibited brewers from using ingredients other than hops, malt, water and yeast in the brewing process. Many foreign beers contain additional ingredients such as sugars or fruit, and so the German authorities have restricted their sale. It has now been decided that this practice is in conflict with EEC law and must be discontinued. Other German labelling regulations will probably suffer the same fate in the future.

10
FINANCING

10.1 Introduction

The world of finance has become increasingly international in nature, such that the German law which governs debts and loans is very similar to the laws of the United Kingdom in many respects, with only cheques and bills of exchange being governed by slightly different rules. Hire purchase agreements and leasing contracts, which originate in the Anglo-American legal system, have been integrated into German law with very little change.

Businessmen attempting to raise finance have three main sources open to them:

(1) Loans, from banks, buildings society savings plans and private loans.
(2) Bills of exchange.
(3) Leasing, in the form of operating or finance leases.

The businessman can find himself on both sides of a financing contract. He will need loans to finance his company and he will probably grant credit to his customers. Both aspects of the law of finance shall be examined in the following chapter.

10.2 Loans

The statutory law dealing with loans in Germany consists of only a few rules. Therefore, banks and buildings societies regulate loans in their general terms of business. These terms are subject to abuse control by the bank supervising authority. Additionally, individual contractual provisions can be declared void by the German courts.

Whilst compound interest is clearly prohibited by the law, provisions concerning high interest rates have been subject to much legal argument. While private individuals are very well protected by a new consumer loans law, businessmen find themselves in a more difficult position. The most important points which have to be taken into consideration when concluding a loans contract will be examined below.

10.2.1 CONCLUSION OF A LOANS CONTRACT

Basically, a loans contract may be concluded informally. In practice, the borrower usually has to confirm a carefully worded 'loan opening letter' in writing. Furthermore, the promise to grant securities on real estate such as a *Hypothek*, *Grundschuld* (see Chapter 6) must be contained in a notarial document.

Loans can be obtained from banks, mortgage banks, building societies and private individuals.

10.2.2 BUILDING SOCIETY SAVINGS PLANS

German building societies usually offer a savings plan, which enables the borrower to obtain a loan at a very low interest rate. This is achieved in two steps: first, the borrower undertakes to pay a monthly sum to the building society until his account has reached an agreed amount (say DM 20,000). These savings will carry little or no interest (maybe 2 per cent). Subsequently, double the saved amount will be released to the borrower, who will only have to pay a fixed interest rate of currently (1991) 4.5 per cent on the loan. These savings plans are subsidised and mainly available to private borrowers. However, they have recently become available for a restricted number of commercial purposes as well.

10.2.3 PRIVATE LOANS

Company loans which are obtained from private individuals can be subject to certain restrictions, if the creditor has a personal interest in the business. So-called capital replacing loans to a GmbH or AG may be treated as part of the company's capital stock if a similar loan could not have been obtained on the credit market. Loans which a shareholder grants to his company are particularly affected by this rule. It is considered dishonest to provide a loan rather than fresh capital to a company in times of crisis.

10.2.4 Terms and Conditions

Banks usually pay out 90 to 98 per cent of the loan amount. Cancellation fees of about 4.5 per cent can be charged if the loan is not called for. Only building societies pay out the full amount.

Usury

Article 138 of the Civil Code prohibits profiteering. The charge of excessive interest rates is considered immoral, and renders the entire loans contract void.

Sophisticated rules determine the borderline between high interest rates and usury. Two main tests exist, based on the average market rate which is represented by the official interest rates set by the German Bundesbank.

The first test asks whether a particular interest rate exceeds double the official rate, so if the official rate is 11 per cent, the limit for high interest rates is 22 per cent.

The second test sets an absolute limit to interest charges by demanding that the market rate must not be exceeded by more than 12 absolute points, so with a market rate of 11 per cent, the limit is 11 + 12 points = 23 per cent.

Matters are complicated further if arrangement fees are charged or life insurance is required. All such additional expense has to be taken into consideration when calculating the true interest rate. As a result, the validity of some types of loan contracts can only be established by a qualified mathematician.

Advice

If a bank gains a particularly strong influence over the management of a company as a consequence of a loans contract, certain consultation obligations on behalf of the company can result. If the bank fails to meet those obligations, it can be held liable for damages.

Value clauses

To protect a loan against inflation, the total payment is often bound to a stable value, such as the gold price. Such clauses are called value clauses. The approval of the German *Bundesbank* is needed to validify such clauses, because their frequent use accelerates inflation.

10.2.5 SECURITIES

The reader of this book will no doubt know that banks do not grant loans without securities. Major loans are usually secured by means of a mortgage, but company equipment such as machines, cars and stored goods can also be used to secure a loan.

Mortgages

Mortgages exist in the form of a *Hypothek* or a *Grundschuld* (see Chapter 6.)

A *Hypothek* is used to secure long-term loans, which are repaid in regular monthly instalments. It is frequently used to secure building society loans.

A *Grundschuld* is used to secure flexible loans that vary considerably in size and duration. As the requirements for their creation have already been described in Chapter 6, this chapter will only deal with certain financial points of interest regarding mortgages.

Interim financing. A *Hypothek* can be issued in two different forms; the registered and the deed form. While a registered *Hypothek* can only be transferred through registration, a deed-based *Hypothek* can be transferred by means of conveying ownership in the deed document. This makes it possible to finance interim periods between the receipt of a large loan amount and the commencement of a project. The bank, which provides interim monies, is assigned the deed document as a security. It will then release the interim monies to the debtor. Once the final loan is received, the interim monies are repaid with part of this sum and the deed document is now returned.

This peculiar system owes its existence to the fact that a *Hypothek* is an accessory right which lives and dies with the money claim that it secures. The empty shell of the *Hypothek* which exists before a loan has been paid out, is at the free disposition of the owner of the mortgaged land, until he has received his monies.

Repossession. If the debtor fails to repay the loan, the mortgagor can sell the mortgaged land by way of public auction. To initiate an auction, he has to obtain judgment against the debtor. In the auction, the mortgagor can bid for the land himself, in which case the amount of money he is owed will be set off against the purchase price.

Security on assets other than land

Other than real estate, a commercial company usually has two additional valuable assets:

(1) Claims against customers.
(2) Unsold goods and company equipment.

The traditional way of granting such assets as security is the lien. However, liens have several severe disadvantages under German law, which have led to the creation of a hybrid lien which is called *Sicherungsübereignung*.

Security on movable objects. Since German law only knows a possessory lien, it is impossible to grant a lien on an object and retain possession of that object at the same time. As a result, machines or goods would have to be removed from the business premises of the debtor to create a valid lien. Obviously, this solution is impracticable and, therefore, a modern hybrid security was invented. To create this security, the debtor has to transfer the title in the goods to his creditor for security purposes, who then lends the goods back to his debtor free of charge, so that the debtor does not lose possession of the goods. The creditor is under a contractual obligation to return the title in the goods to the debtor as soon as the loan has been repaid. This method is now universally accepted and has practically replaced the possessory lien. It requires clear description of all goods transferred in a skilfully worded security contract. Professional advice should therefore be sought.

Security in rights. A lien can also exist on rights such as debt claims or claims for damages. However, the person granting the lien must notify his debtor in writing that he has granted a lien on the claim. The performance of this duty is perceived as damaging to reputation and creditworthiness, and so the *Sicherungszession* was invented. This is a security transaction which involves the nominal assignment of claims against a third party to the creditor. The creditor then grants the debtor permission to collect the debts. Thus notification can be avoided and, if all goes well, nobody will ever know about the credit arrangement.

10.3 Leasing

Leasing contracts have quickly gained wide popularity in Germany, although legally, their Anglo-American origins give rise to several difficulties. Two types of leasing contracts, the finance and operating lease, are known in Germany, and their contents vary according to the kind of object leased. One can lease virtually anything, although this generally applies to machines, cars or real estate.

10.3.1 FINANCE LEASING

Finance leasing is the most common form of leasing. It is, roughly speaking, a hire-purchase type of contract, which is characterised by long rental periods (three to seven years) with an option to purchase the leased goods at the end of that period. The lessor can either be the manufacturer of the leased object, or a finance company who refinances the leasing project with a bank. In this case, the bank will often receive security rights over the leased goods. The lessee contractually undertakes the maintenance and the insurance of a leased object. In many respects, he has the same obligations as a full proprietor with regard to the leased object.

Damage to the leased goods

Problems occur if the leased goods suffer damage by third party negligence. The leasing contract will usually oblige the lessee to carry out all necessary repairs and assign the lessor's right to claim compensation to the lessee. If the third party cannot be traced or cannot afford to pay, the lessee will have to bear the financial risk.

Faulty goods

The lessor usually excludes his liability for hidden faults of the leased goods contractually. He assigns his rights to claim compensation from the manufacturer to the lessee. Such clauses are valid. Again, the lessee bears the risks of legal action and recovery.

Termination

Termination of a finance leasing contract is restricted during the initial rental period. The contract will usually state special circumstances under which the goods can be repossessed — the most common being a failure to pay two or more instalments. At the end of the rental period, the lessee can either choose to terminate the agreement or to purchase the object or prolong the hire period. In the case of termination, all rent paid is lost and the goods have to be returned. Clauses which provide for additional penalties are void.

10.3.2 Operating leasing

Operating leasing is a type of financing contract used for short rental periods. It caters for cases where it is unclear whether the lessee wishes to purchase the leased objects. German courts tend to perceive operating leasing as a type of renting and apply Art 535ff of the BGB to such contracts.

10.3.3 Real estate leasing

Real estate is leased by means of finance leasing with a very long rental period of 30 years or more. The right to purchase the land at the end of the period is secured in the Land Registry by means of a 'notice of purchase' or a 'registered right of pre-emption' (see Chapter 6.)

10.4 Giving credit to customers

The businessman can also stand on the other side of a financing agreement by being the creditor, who agrees to accept payment in instalments. Most vendors of valuable goods cannot expect to receive the purchase price in one lump sum. The following points have to be observed when granting credit to others.

10.4.1 Consumer credit

The consumer credit law seeks to protect the private consumer by setting out special formal requirements which have to be observed when granting credit in excess of DM 400. This law affects most department stores, electrical shops and other businesses which sell expensive products on a consumer credit basis. Simple loans are covered just as well as leasing contracts and credit arrangements on a hire-purchase basis. The main requirements which must be observed are:

(1) There must be a written contract.
(2) The true annual interest rate inclusive of all costs and fees

must be shown. For example, when granting a loan of DM 10,000 for one year at an interest rate of 12 per cent with DM 100 arrangement fee, DM 500 insurance premium and DM 100 costs for handling, the effective annual interest has to be shown at 19 per cent.

(3) Repayment conditions must be set out. Thus, in the above example, monthly repayments have to be shown at DM 991.67.

(4) The total sum of all repayments must be shown. In the above example, the sum of DM 11,900 has to be shown.

Additionally, the consumer has the right to revoke the loan contract. This right must be exercised within one week from the day when the consumer was advised in writing about his right to revoke. To avoid endless possibilities of revocation, a notice of consumer rights which has to be signed separately should be concluded in every credit contract.

10.4.2 THIRD PARTY FINANCE

Finally, another peculiarity concerning loans must be mentioned. It is the so-called third party finance transaction. This term refers to cases where the vendor arranges a loan through his bank for the purchaser. The vendor and the credit institute are perceived as one party under these circumstances, and so the customer can defend his position against the credit institute by means of objections concerning the purchase contract and the quality of the goods.

10.4.3 RETENTION OF TITLE

When selling movable objects, the best way to secure the claim for payment is a retention of title. To achieve a retention of title, a clause has to be entered into the purchase contract, which reserves the property in the goods with the vendor until the full purchase price has been paid. If the customer needs to work with or re-sell the goods, permission is usually granted to do so in the due course of business.

11
INSOLVENCY AND ENFORCEMENT

11.1 Introduction

German legal procedure is traditionally divided into two distinct sections: obtaining a title and enforcement.

It is a sad fact of commercial life that a glorious legal victory can be of little value if the debtor is unable or unwilling to pay. It may be that he is in financial difficulties and on the verge of bankruptcy, in which case an insolvency procedure has to be initiated.

The debtor may simply be trying to delay payment, which means that a normal enforcement procedure should be commenced. It must be noted that enforcement is not possible once insolvency proceedings have been initiated. All other legal proceedings are interrupted until an administrator or liquidator has been appointed. Unsecured creditors will usually have little hope of receiving more than five to ten per cent of their claims once this stage has been reached. It is, therefore, advisable for unsecured creditors to attempt individual enforcement rather than insolvency procedures, in order to realise their claim.

11.2 Enforcement

The law of enforcement is contained in Art 704ff of the Code of Civil Procedures. It deals with the possibilities open to an individual creditor attempting to enforce a claim.

11.2.1 Title

A creditor who wishes to enforce a debt first needs to obtain an enforceable title. The following enforceable titles are most commonly encountered.

) The creditor may object against the refusal to enforce a title (such as if the bailiff refuses to seize an object), or may issue a writ of conference to transfer a title to someone else (for example, if the heir of a creditor wishes to enforce a title).

) A third party may issue a writ of contradiction against the seizure of an asset (as in the case of the seizure of third party property), or issue a writ of priority to ensure the full satisfaction of a claim (if, for example, a second creditor wishes to claim priority).

In addition to the above, 'reminders' are available against all ecisions of a clerk or a bailiff to the judge in chambers.

1.2.4 LOCATING HIDDEN ASSETS

Experienced debtors resort to skilful ways and means of iding assets from their creditors. Therefore, a number of nethods exist to discover hidden assets.

)ath of Manifestation

A disappointed creditor can force his debtor to swear an)ath of Manifestation. The debtor has to appear before the Court and answer a number of questions on his financial situation such as, whether he owns a house, a car, or receives a salary?). Additionally he will be entered on the so-called 'list of debtors', which is very much feared by commercial men, since anyone ntered on the list of debtors is virtually uncreditworthy.

A sudden willingness to pay may result from such action.

Bank accounts

It is always worth effecting the seizure of all bank accounts of debtor as this will make it impossible for him to use his bank for urther financial transactions. If he is still trading actively, this will inconvenience him considerably.

Some courts will also permit the seizure of a credit line, so that as soon as the debtor calls for a credit, the monies will have to be released to the creditor. However, it has to be noted that this procedure is not undisputed and will not be upheld by all courts.

SCHUFA

The SCHUFA is a well known private organisation which maintains blacklists of uncreditworthy persons and companies. For a small membership fee, information on the reputation of a

(1) A judgment — which can be either provisional or final.
(2) A notarial document containing an enforcement clause.
(3) An injunction.
(4) An enforcement order for foreign titles.
(5) A court settlement.

Unlike the case in the UK, the possibility of an appeal prevents enforceability of a judgment. However, a judgment can be declared provisionally enforceable by the court, if certain conditions are met. As a rule security has to be given in this event. Default judgments and judgments against which an appeal is possible are the most important provisionally enforceable titles.

If the debtor is already in financial difficulties, a creditor will be well advised to provide security and commence enforcement immediately. Security can usually be given by bank guarantee with leave of the court.

Foreign title

To enforce a foreign title it is necessary to obtain a court order, using one of the following procedures:

(1) Judgment procedure: on the condition that the title is enforceable, not contrary to the *ordre public* and has guarantee of mutuality, foreign judgments can be declared enforceable by judgment.
(2) By declaration: foreign judgments can be declared enforceable by means of a simple declaration on the condition that an international treaty provides for this procedure.
(3) By certificate: if a European agreement concerning enforcement of judgment applies, a simple certificate of enforceability will suffice.

Other titles

A settlement is an enforceable title, if it has been concluded before a judge in court. The settlement has to be reached after legal proceedings were commenced, in which case the settlement terminates the proceedings and replaces a judgment. The settlement is a fully enforceable title.

Injunctions are also enforceable by their very nature, but they are merely temporary measures of enforcement, which can be undone if proceedings are not commenced within 14 days or if the debtor can show cause.

Furthermore, the debtor can submit to immediate enforcement of a debt by signing a notarial document to this effect. The document needs to set out the exact amount due and the conditions of enforcement.

Various other titles are listed in Art 794 of the Code of Civil Procedure.

11.2.2 METHODS OF ENFORCEMENT

Once an enforceable title has been obtained, it has to be stamped by the court and served on the debtor. The creditor now has the difficult task of instructing the bailiff. To instruct the bailiff successfully the creditor will need to know whether the debtor has any valuable assets and where to locate them.

Movable assets

Movable assets are seized by the bailiff by means of sealing them. It is always worth sending the bailiff to the debtor's address to investigate whether expensive items such as a new video recorder or camera have been purchased that could be seized. However, this is rare and the success rate of such seizures is low. The reason for this is that most debtors have skilful ways to ensure that the bailiff will not find any valuable objects which would be worth seizing, although the occasional find can be made.

Attachment of earnings orders and other garnishee proceedings

A more promising method of enforcement are garnishee orders attaching claims and rights which the debtor has against third parties. Monetary claims can be seized by a court order. To obtain such an order the creditor needs to fill in a prescribed form setting out the nature of the claim which he believes that his debtor has against a third party. The court will then order the third party to pay the amount owed to the creditor rather than to the debtor. The third party can refuse to pay, in which case the creditor will have to sue him.

Claims for salaries or wages are amongst the rights which are most commonly seized. Their seizure is usually successful, though individual debtors are entitled to various allowances, which cannot be touched. The procedure is similar to that used in the UK for obtaining an attachment of earnings order.

Real estate

Real estate is sold by means of compulsory au
real estate a creditor has to obtain an auction orde
Mortgagors have to obtain a judgment which per
sion and sale of the land. Other creditors have to
enforceable title to the Land Registry, which will e
mortgage on their behalf, which can then be enfor

For smaller sums, enforcement by sequestrat
able. Sequestration is a form of official adminis
estate. The administrator will manage the estate on
creditor and transfer all rent and other earnings whi
to the creditor. This has the additional advan
unsecured creditor can obtain proceeds from real es
of sequestration, while an auction will usually
satisfaction of the mortgagors only. Once all secure
been paid out, the auction proceeds will usually be

11.2.3 PROCEDURE

Enforcement procedure is a very complica
German law. Different officers of the court ha
functions.

Thus, bailiffs deal with the seizure of goods c
enforcement involving the use of force. Appeals
actions of bailiffs are made to the clerk. The clerk als
garnishee orders and attachment of earnings orders an
leave to depart from standard procedure — such as
valuable goods to be sold at private, rather than pub
Appeals against decisions of the clerk are made to t

The system of appeals and other remedies in e
matters is a true legal jungle which should only be exp
experienced litigator.

Special proceedings exist for virtually every field
ment. The issue is further complicated by the fact th
parties have different remedies. To give a brief over
remedies available the following list has been drawn

(1) The debtor has the remedy of raising technical
against any irregularities of procedure or s
objections concerning points of law, of which
must be made by writ.

business contact can be obtained, which may avoid later disappointment. One can also report unreliable debtors to the SCHUFA.

11.3 INSOLVENCY

Persons or companies who have become unable to pay their debts will have to face insolvency procedures. Two procedures exist; the insolvency compromise procedure (*Vergleich*) and the liquidation procedure (*Konkurs*). Both procedures commence with an application for an insolvency order. Directors of corporations are under an obligation to notify the insolvency court of pending insolvency as soon as it becomes clear that the company's capital stock has been exhausted. Other insolvency procedures commence upon application by a creditor. The creditor has to show to the court that the debtor is unable to pay his debts. Unsuccessful attempts of enforcement often serve as proof for this.

The court will refuse to order liquidation if there are no sufficient funds to cover the costs of appointing a liquidator and paying his fees. In this case the company is simply deleted from the Companies Registry.

The German system of insolvency distinguishes between companies and private individuals: Corporations (AG, GmbH, GmbH & Co, KG) become insolvent when either the capital stock becomes exhausted or they are unable to pay their debts. In such an instance, the managing director has to make an application for insolvency. Such application can also be made by any creditor.

Individuals (sole traders) and partnerships (OHG, KG) become insolvent when they are unable to pay their debts. Applications for insolvency can be made by any creditor or by the debtor himself.

In both cases, three types of procedure are available:

(1) The insolvency compromise procedure.
(2) The liquidation procedure.
(3) Deletion from the Companies Registry due to insufficient assets.

More than 80 per cent of all applications for insolvency procedures do not lead to liquidation, because there are insufficient funds to cover costs after the secured creditors have made use of their security rights. It is, therefore, very important to secure claims and to know about the ranking of securities within the system of German insolvency law. The following section will deal with various commercially important problems of security rights and the ranking of creditors in insolvency law.

11.3.1 LIQUIDATION PROCEDURE

The procedure for liquidation under German law consists of various phases.

Firstly, a court order must be applied for. The application can either be made by a creditor or the owner of a company. If the application is successful, the court order will be publicised and registered. As a next step a liquidator will be appointed by the court, with the appointment also being publicised. The liquidator will then ask all creditors to notify him in writing of any claims they may have against the company. All such claims are put on a list, which is presented to all creditors who may raise objections against these claims to prevent them from becoming absolute. Disputed claims are subject to a special verification procedure. If they are verified, they will participate in the distribution of the remaining assets together with undisputed claims.

11.3.2 COMPOSITION

The composition procedure is very similar to the liquidation procedure. It also commences upon application, which can either be made by a creditor or by the owner of a company. The application needs to be supported by various documents and needs to contain a detailed suggestion on how to save the company by compounding the company debts. If the court can be convinced that the scheme suggested is viable it will make a Composition Order, and appoint an administrator. These orders are published. The administrator will then call a meeting of all unsecured creditors. If those creditors reach an agreement to the effect that they will forego a certain percentage of their claims in order to ensure the survival of the company, the company will be allowed to continue trading. If no such agreement can be reached subsequent liquidation will ensue which will result in the deletion of the company from the Companies Registry and possibly in a loss of 80 to 90 per cent of all claims. A good compromise between creditors and a company will ensure that the creditors receive between 30–50 per cent of the monies which they are owed. Rates below 20 per cent are usually refused by the court as insufficient. The case is then referred to liquidation.

11.3.3 RANKING OF CREDITORS

When examining the rank of creditors of a company which is in liquidation, a distinction needs to be made between secured and unsecured creditors. Some secured creditors are not concerned with the liquidation procedure as such, because their security rights allow them to repossess certain assets. These creditors are called 'real creditors'. Other groups of creditors are given priority over ordinary claims for political and social reasons. They are called 'privileged creditors'. Still another group of creditors has a right of preferential satisfaction, while others come last of the list. The various groups of creditors which exist and their ranking are considered below.

Real creditors

Strictly speaking, a real creditor is not involved in liquidation proceedings, because his security right gives him a full title to the goods involved. He simply repossesses the secured items and sells them, and does not need to share the proceeds of the sale with any other creditors. Obviously this is a very desirable position to be in, and can be achieved by suppliers of goods and materials by means of retention of title (see Chapter 10) or by creditors who have obtained a *Sicherungsübereignung* (see Section 10.2.5).

However, the liquidator can avoid repossession by paying the debt which is owed to a real creditor, in which case the security right is terminated. The liquidator will choose to do so if the amount owed is considerably lower than the value of the repossessed item.

Creditors with a right to preferential satisfaction

A further category of creditors is entitled to preferential satisfaction, meaning that they may separate certain objects from the remaining company assets and satisfy their claims out of the proceeds obtained from the sale. However, other than in the case of real creditors, any surplus monies which remain have to be returned to the liquidator who will distribute them amongst the other creditors.

Creditors entitled to preferential satisfaction include all mortgagors (*Hypothek* and *Grundschuld*), holders of liens and hybrid liens (see Section **10.2.5**). The correct treatment of a *Sicherungsübereignung* is in dispute in this respect. Some perceive it as a full legal title, while others advocate treatment as if a *Sicherungsübereignung* was a lien.

Set-offs

Unsecured creditors against whom the bankrupt party has a counterclaim can use their right to a set-off. Parties who are indebted to an insolvent company can also make use of this privilege if they acquired their counterclaim before the liquidation order was publicised. Unliquidated counterclaims and counterclaims concerning specific performance will be converted into liquidated amounts for this purpose.

Notice of purchase

A notice of purchase (see Section **6.2.2**) secures the right of a buyer of real estate to the property which he has purchased. If he has paid the purchase price to the vendor, which is now in liquidation, but his name has not yet been registered, he can demand that the liquidator transfers the property title to him and agrees to registration.

Privileged creditors

Once the above creditors have been paid, a fairly meagre amount of money will remain, which is usually consumed to pay up the so-called 'liquidator-debts'. These debts are monies owing to creditors who have contracted with the liquidator after the liquidation order was made, such as electricity and water suppliers who have no choice but to continue delivering their services.

Second priority is given to outstanding salaries and pension payments for social reasons. These claims are paid out before any commercial creditors receive money.

Unsecured creditors

The remaining creditors rank according to political considerations. Tax bills and other official fees and costs take priority over ordinary claims.

11.3.4 BANKRUPTCY OF THE INSOLVENCY LAWS

German bankruptcy law has experienced much controversial discussion recently. Reform has been shown to be well overdue, since the increase of security rights has led to the result that the vast majority of unsecured creditors receive nothing. Over 80 per cent of all applications for insolvency proceedings are currently rejected because there are not enough funds to cover the cost once all security rights have been exercised. As a result, the German Insolvency Law is practically ineffective for those who have not obtained sufficient security. The slogan being used to describe this situation is the 'Bankruptcy of Bankruptcy'.

Hopefully reforms will soon be implemented.

LEGISLATION TABLE

German Legislation — *Page*

AGBG (Unfair Contract Terms Law)
- art 9 87

Building Ordinance 125

Civil Code (BGB)
- art 12 .... 22, 25
- art 138 136
- art 242 87
- art 419 78
- arts 459–480 79
- art 535ff 98, 140
- art 611(*a*) 113
- art 613(*a*) 74, 110
- art 823 .... 22, 26
  - r2 26
- art 930 93
- art 931 93

Code of Civil Procedures
- art 704ff 142
- art 794 144

Commercial Code (HGB)
- art 1 53
- art 17 .... 22, 26
- art 25 .... 77, 78
- arts 94–97 86
- art 119 56
- art 124 56
- arts 170–75 57

Copyright Law 14, 17, 18

Environmental Liability Law 131

Federal Building Law 125
- arts 29–36 126

Federal Water Law
- art 22 130

German Constitution
- art 1 18
- art 2 18
- art 3 113

GWB (Law Prohibiting Restraints on Competition) 27, 35–37
arts 15–18 87
art 18. 87
art 25(1) 39
art 26. 48
GWEB (Cartels Law) 37–39
Insolvency Law 151
Law Governing Public Limited Companies
art 93. 67
Medical Products Liability Law 131
Patent Law
art 3. 8
art 4. 8
Products Liability Law 131
Registered Designs Law. 15
art 14(*a*) 16
Road Traffic Act 131
Utility Patent law
art 1. 11
UWG (Law of Unfair Competition). 27–34
art 1. 29–31
art 3. . . . . 29, 31
art 6(*a*) 29
(*b*) 29
art 7(*b*) 29
(*c*). 29
(*d*) 29
art 9. 29
art 12. 29
art 14. 29
art 15. 29
art 16. . . . . 7, 22, 26
art 17. . . . . 7, 22, 26, 29
Waste Law
art 22. 130
WZG (Trademark Law). 22
art 22. 23

European Community Legislation
Directive 84/450/EEC (Advertising Directive). 34
Directive 85/2137/EEC 69
art 40. 69
Regulation 67/67/EEC. 45, 47
Regulation 4087/88/EEC. 89
Treaty of Rome
art 85. . . . . 28, 36, 41, 45, 89
(3) 42
art 86. . . . . 28, 36

INDEX

Acquisitions. *See* Mergers and acquisitions
Agency—
branch system, 82
brokers, 85–6
duties, 86
rights, 86
commercial representatives, 82–5
company's duties, 83–4
relationship to company, 82–3
rights and duties, 83
commission agents, 85
disclosed, 81
dispute settlement, 85
European law, 84
foreign law, 84
general representative, 84
termination, 84
third party relationships, 84
undisclosed, 81
See also Franchise contracts; Home traders

Brokers. *See* Agency
Building law. *See* Environmental and planning law
Business organisation—
categories, 52–3
See also Limited companies; Partnerships; Sole traders

Cartels, 35–51
authorities, 36
categories of agreements, 37–8
decartelisation, 36
definition, 38–41
company, 38
exempted, 38–9

Cartels—*contd.*
contract, 39
European law, 40–41
manipulation of market, 39–40
restriction of competition, 40
domination of market, 47–9
abuse of market power, 47
courses of action, 48–9
concessions, demand for, 49
delivery blockades, 49
dependent companies, 49
dominance defined, 47–8
European law, 48–9
European law on, 36, 46–7
GWB, 36
horizontal agreements, 37
joint ventures, 41
privileged, 41–3
block exemptions (European law), 42–3
exempted groups, 41–2
notification, 42
procedures, 36–7
actions for injured parties, 37
formal procedure, 37
preliminary investigation, 36–7
vertical agreements, 37–8, 43–6
European law, 45–6
distribution systems, 45
licensing, 45–6
exclusivity ties, 43
package deals, 44
supplementary goods, purchase and sale of, 44
third party dealings (distribution ties), 44
licensing contracts, 45
price ties, 43

Cartels—*contd.*
  See also Mergers and acquisitions
Civil procedure, 5
Commentaries, 2
Commercial property—
  protection of, 7
  registration of protective rights, 7
  See also Copyright; Patents; Registered Designs; Trademarks; Utility patents
Competition law—
  development of law, 27
  EEC law, influence of, 27–8
  See also Cartels, Mergers and acquisitions; Unfair competition
Copyright, 16–21
  access to work, 19
  characteristics, 16–17
  creative merit, 17
  expiry of, 19–20
  exploitation rights, 18–19
  graphic art, 17
  individuality, 17
  intellectual content, 17
  law, 16
  photographic work and films, 18
  protection offered, 18–19
    personality rights, 18
  reproduction rights, 20
  royalties, 19
  scientific work, 18
  spoken works of art, 17
  transfers of, 20
    exploitation societies, 21
    GEMA (authors' and musicians' society), 21
    publishing contract, 20–21
  violation, protection against, 19
Costs, 6
Courts—
  administrative, 4
  civil, 3–4
    Amtsgericht, 3
    appeals, 3
      Bundesgerichtshof, 3
      Oberlandes gericht, 3
    choice of forum, 3
    Landsgericht, 3
Courts—*contd.*
  constitutional, 4
  labour, 4
Credit. *See* Financing

Employment law, 104–13
  discrimination, 113
  employee co-determination, 110–11
    management level, 111
    workers' council, 110–11
  employment contracts, 105–7
    employees, 105
    handicapped persons, 106
    hazardous work, 106–7
    indefinite period, 105
    paid holidays, 106
    salary and social insurance, 105–6
    sick pay, 106
    termination, 107–10
      extraordinary notice, by, 108
      ordinary notice, by, 107–8
  labour courts, 109–10, 113
  labour laws, 104
  termination
    agreement, by, 110
    sale of business, on, 110
    unfair dismissal, protection against, 108–10
      labour court, actions in, 109–10
      social justification, 108–9
      special protection, 109
  trade unions and collective bargaining, 111–13
    area of application, 112
    lock-outs, 112–13
    priority rule, 112
    strikes, 112
Enforcement—
  bank accounts, 146
  locating hidden assets, 146–7
  methods of, 144–5
    attachment of earnings, 144
    garnishee proceedings, 144
    movable assets, 144
    real estate, 145

Enforcement—*contd.*
  oath of manifestation, 146
  procedure, 145–6
  SCHUFA, 146–7
  title, 142–4
    compromise, 143
    foreign, 143
    injunctions, 143
    submission to enforcement, 143–4
  See also Insolvency
Environmental and planning law, 124–33
  building law, 126–7
    building areas, 126
    building ordinance, 126–7
    large projects, 127
    neighbour rights, 127
    procedure, 127
  environmental liability law, 130–32
    damage caused, 132
    European law, 132
    hazardous plants, 131
    liability, 131
    limitation of liability, 132
  environmental protection, 128–9
    licensing, 128–9
      formalised procedure, 128
      partial licences, 129
      requirements, 128–9
      simplified procedure, 128
    unlicensed businesses, control of, 129
  product labelling, 132–3
    cosmetics, 133
    European law, 133
    foodstuffs, 132–3
  public law, 124–5
    administrative law, 124–5
    administrative orders, 125
    federal and non-federal laws, 125
  waste disposal law, 130
    private waste disposal, 130
  water law, 129–30
    licensing, 129–30

Financing—
  credit, 140–41
    consumer credit law, 140–41
    retention of title, 141
    third party finance, 141
  leasing contracts, 138–40
    finance leasing, 139–40
      damage to leased goods, 139
      faulty goods, 139
      termination, 139–40
    operating leasing, 140
    real estate leasing, 140
  loans, 134–8
    advice, 136
    building society savings plans, 135
    conclusion of loan contract, 135
    interest, 136
    mortgages, 137. *See also* Property law
      Grundschuld, 137
      Hypothek, 137
      interim financing, 137
      repossession, 137
    private, 135
    securities, 137–8
      movable objects, on, 138
      rights, in, 138
    terms and conditions, 136
    value clauses, 136
  sources of business loans, 134
Franchise contracts—
  applicable law, 87–8
  defined, 86–7
  European law, 89
  industrial property, protection for, 88
  termination, 88
  See also Home traders

Home traders, 89–91
  defined, 89–90
  protection of, 90–91
  supplier, relationship with, 90

Immigration, 103–4
  EEC nationals, 104
  non-EEC nationals, 103–4

Insolvency, 147–51
  companies, 147
  compromise procedure (*Vergleich*), 147
  individuals, 147
  ineffectiveness of law, 151
  liquidation procedure (*Konkurs*), 147, 148–9
  ranking of creditors, 149–50
    notice of purchase, 150
    preferential satisfaction, 149–50
    privileged creditors, 150
    real creditors, 149
    set-offs, 150
    unsecured creditors, 150
  See also Enforcement
Intellectual property. *See* Commercial property
Interpretation of the law, 1

Labels, protection of. *See* Trademarks
Lawyers—
  fee structure code ('BRAGO'), 5–6
  Rechtsanwälte, 5
  representation at court, 5
Leasing contracts. *See* Financing
Limited companies—
  disclosure provisions, 70–71
  EEIG (European Economic Industry Grouping), 69–70
    formation, 69
    liability, 69
    representation and structure, 69
    taxation, 69–70
  foreign, setting up branches, 91
  GmbH (private), 61–4
    capital requirements, 61–2
    company name, 62–3
    formation procedures, 62
    liabilities, 63
    organisation, 63
    sale of shares, 63
    taxation and costs, 63–4
  public (AG)
    company name, 66
    formation procedure, 64–6
    internal structure, 66–7

Limited companies—*contd.*
      board of directors, 66
      general meeting, 67
      supervisory board, 66–7
    liability, 67–8
    quoted, 64
    sale of shares, 68
    taxation, 68
  VVaG and eG (mutual insurance companies), 68–9
  See also Mergers and acquisitions

Mergers and acquisitions—
  fusion control, 49–51
  guarantees
    contractual, 80
    general law, 79–80
  limited companies
    fiscal considerations, 76
    GmbH (private) shares and stocks, 79
    letter of intent, 77
    liability, 77–9
      company name, continuation of, 77–8
      private debts of vendor (Art 419), 78
      unpaid taxes, 78
    licences, 76
    supervision by Cartels' Authority, 76
  notification procedure, 51
  partnerships
    general partner's share, 78
    limited, 78–9
  procedures, 72
  purchase of assets, 73–5
    company as whole, 75
    employees, 74
    industrial property rights, 74
    liabilities, transfer of, 74
    negative limitation, 73–5
      private assets, 73
      unwanted assets, 73
    positive description, 74
  purchase of company, 72–3
  purchase of holding, 75
    limited companies

Mergers and acquisitions—*contd.*
formalities, 75
partnerships, 75
See also Cartels
Monopolies. *See* Cartels

Names, protection of. *See* Trademarks
Notaries, 6

Partnerships, 53, 55–61
benefits and drawbacks, 57, 59–60
disclosure provisions, 70–71
general, 55–7
death of partner, 101–2
formation, 55–6
liability, 56–7
representation, 56
sale of share, 57
taxation, 57
trading name, 56
limited, 57–60
formation procedures, 58
general partner's liability, 57
liability, 59
mass partnerships, 58
representation, 58
taxation, 59
trading name, 58
silent, 60–61
formation, 60
liability, 60
taxation, 60–61
See also Mergers and acquisitions
Patents—
applicant, 10
application, formal requirements, 9
examination, 9
fees, 10
foreign, 8
inspection of files, 10
novelty, 8
objections, 10
obvious flaws, 9–10
patentable inventions, 8
period of protection, 8
procedural law, 9–10
Patents—*contd.*
remedies against registration, 10–11
action for recovery, 11
appeal, 11
further and more detailed examination, 11
novelty examination, 10–11
revocation, 11
specialist courts and lawyers, 7
utility, 8–9
See also Copyright; Registered designs
Product labelling. *See* Environmental and planning law
Property law, 92–9
abstraction, doctrine of, 92
business leases, 98–9
entire business leases (*Pacht*), 99
leasing business premises (*Miete*), 98–9
co-property, 98
leasehold interest, 97–8
movables, 93–4
promissory contract, 92, 93
purchase in good faith, 94
security rights and reservations, 94
transfer of ownership, 93–4
real property
defined, 94
Land Registry, functions of, 96
mortgages, 96–7. *See also* Financing
mortgagee's rights and remedies, 97
proprietor's own (*Eigentümergrundschuld*), 97
purchase procedure, 95–6
true owner's objection, 96
See also Succession
Public law. *See* Environmental and planning law

Registered designs, 14–16
appeals, 16
laws, 14
procedure, 15–16

Registered designs—*contd.*
collective application, 15
deadline, 15
fee, 16
written application, 15
remedies, 16
requirements for registration, 14–15
models, 15
novelty, 15
originality, 15
patterns, 15
scope of protection, 16
work protected, 14

Schönfelder (compilation of civil code), 1–2
Sole traders, 53–5
formation procedure, 54
liability, 54
minor and major distinction, 53–4
registration, 53
representation, 54
sale of business, 55
taxation, 55
trading name, 54
Sources of law, 1–2
Succession, 99–102
arbitrary, 100–101
two-sided testament, 100–101
wills, 100
business, 101–2
contractual solutions, 101
testamentary solutions, 101–2
inheritance tax, 102. *See also* Inheritance tax
statutory, 100
types of, 100–102

Taxation law, 114–23
direct taxes, 115–20
appeals, 115
calculations, 116
capital tax, 118–19
double taxation, 119
corporation tax, 117–18
deductions, 118

Taxation law—*contd.*
dividend cash-back procedure, 117
emigration of company, 118
profits assessable, 117
income tax, 115
inheritance tax, 119–20
allowances, 119
incidence of, 119
procedure, 120
rates, 119
trade tax, 120
double taxation agreements, 114–15
federal and state, 114
foreigners' liability, 114
indirect taxes, 120–23
locally levied, 123
value added tax, 121–2
procedure, 121–2
taxable transactions, 121
taxpaper, 121
special contributions, 123
Trademarks, 21–6
definition, 22
collective, 23
defensive, 23
description of origin, 23
free, 23
identifier of goods, 22–3
packaging and get-up, 23
visible to eye, 22
deletion if not used, 23
goodwill protection, 25–6
business secrets (Article 17 UWG), 26
company names (Article 16 UWG) 26
negligent violation (Article 823 Civil Code), 26
right of name (Article 12 BGB), 25–6
trading names (Article 17 Commercial Code), 26
law, 21–2
objection procedure, 25
priority rule, 23–4

Trademarks—*contd.*
    similarity of products (test 1), 24
    similarity of symbols (test 2), 24
  protection, scope of, 25
  registration procedure, 24–5
  remedies, 25

Unfair competition (UWG), 28–35
  Article 1, 29–31
    breach of law, 31
    exploitation of others' achievements, 30–31
    headhunting, 31
    market disturbance, 31
    passing off, 30
    poaching customers, 30
    unfair hindrance, 30
  Article 3, 31–4
    advertising techniques, 31
    deceit, 32–3
    European advertising directive (84/450), effect of, 34
    medical advertising, 33
    misleading statements, 31–2
    price deception, 33
    sales, misrepresentations about, 33–4
Unfair competition—*contd.*
    superlative advertising, 34
  compensation claims, 35
  competitive situations, 29
  discontinuance claims, 35
  general rules, 28–9
  procedural peculiarities, 35
Unification—
  transitional provisions, 2
Utility patents—
  application, 13
  collisions, 14
  double protection, 13
  examination procedure, 13
  inventive requirements, 11–12
  movable objects, 12
  new design, 12
  novelty, 12
  procedure, 12–13
  remedies, 13
  useful purpose, 12
  See also Copyrights; Patents; Registered designs

Waste disposal law, 130
Water law. *See* Environmental and planning law